Praise for *The Big Swim*

A stunningly beautiful memoir about a world that I love. Carrie Saxifrage is a poet not just of the natural world but also of the heart, and reading her book is like walking through these landscapes with a wise and knowledgeable guide; with every chapter you turn a corner onto another unexpected and breathtaking vista. She has a keen, compassionate eye for human foibles, and I found myself laughing out loud on one page and brushing away tears on the next. I read straight through. I did not want this journey to end.

— Ruth Ozeki , author, *A Tale for the Time Being*

In a flash of inspiration, Carrie Saxifrage has invented the climate change memoir. Beautifully crafted, often touching and unexpectedly funny, here is your handbook to living deeply in perilous times.

— J.B. MacKinnon, author *The 100-Mile Diet* and *The Once and Future World*

The Big Swim is a riveting read. Carrie Saxifrage takes us with her to some of the West Coast's most precious wild gems while reflecting on parenting, life, love, the beauty around us and its fragility. It's *Eat, Pray, Love* for the climate era. I couldn't put it down.

— Tzeporah Berman, author, *This Crazy Time*

Serious adventure on a serious planet. This is the kind of thinking and living we need to engage in.

— Bill McKibben, author, *Oil and Honey*, *Eaarth* and *The End of Nature*

Trying to understand what we are doing to the planet based solely upon facts and statistics fails to engage the heart, where all true commitment forms. Carrie Saxifrage knows that real change comes from the head and the heart working together and gently pulls us along on her journey to a deeper place of understanding.

— Maude Barlow, National Chairperson, Council of Canadians and author, *Blue Future: Protecting Water for People and the Planet Forever*

Carrie Saxifrage has accomplished a feat here: she's written a story about our pressing environmental concerns that you'll find hard to put down. Funny, intriguing, eloquent, her emotional-intellectual acuity inspires a refreshing sense of volition.

— Betsy Warland, author, *Breathing the Page*

The Big Swim is a beautiful collection of stories about the biggest challenge of our time: How to live with ourselves in a world we are destroying. Carrie Saxifrage writes eloquently about the natural environment and humanity's disruptive place within it. Her insightful blend of science and personal epiphanies will change the way you think.

— Brian Payton, author, *The Wind Is Not a River* and *Shadow of the Bear*

Wow. This moving book invites us to reconnect with our own wildness, to submerge ourselves in creation and come out doused with the sweet nectar of being alive. Carrie Saxifrage speaks a beautiful language—precise, transformative, unafraid. Read this book. It will give you hope.

— Shaena Lambert, author, *Oh, My Darling* and *Radiance*

Carrie Saxifrage looks unflinchingly at the world around us and reports back the joy, the pain, and the adventure that is there, within reach of all those bold individuals who care enough to grasp for it. *The Big Swim* is a must read for all those who think they don't want to read another environmental book. It takes you to a place of hope while step by step you laugh or cry because of the humanity of the parent struggling with a teenager, the spouse working on creating partnership, or the adventurer grasping for the next push forward.

— Manda Aufochs Gillespie, author, *Green Mama*
www.thegreenmama.com

THE
BIG SWIM

Coming Ashore in a World Adrift

Carrie Saxifrage

new society
PUBLISHERS

Cover design by Diane McIntosh.
Swimmer: © iStock/SilviaJansen; Water background:© iStock/davidf;
Ice: © iStock/Sjo; Compass Rose: © iStock /Makhnach_M

Printed in Canada. First printing January 2015.

New Society Publishers acknowledges the financial support
of the Government of Canada through the Canada Book Fund (CBF)
for our publishing activities.

Inquiries regarding requests to reprint all or part of *The Big Swim*
should be addressed to New Society Publishers at the address below.
To order directly from the publishers, please call toll-free
(North America) 1-800-567-6772,
or order online at www.newsociety.com

Any other inquiries can be directed by mail to:
New Society Publishers
P.O. Box 189, Gabriola Island, BC V0R 1X0, Canada
(250) 247-9737

LIBRARY AND ARCHIVES CANADA CATALOGUING IN PUBLICATION

Saxifrage, Carrie, author
The big swim : coming ashore in a world adrift / Carrie Saxifrage.

Issued in print and electronic formats.
ISBN 978-0-86571-798-5 (pbk.). — ISBN 978-1-55092-592-0 (ebook)

1. Saxifrage, Carrie. 2. Environmentalists—British Columbia—
Biography. 3. Journalists—British Columbia—Biography. 4. Philosophy
of nature. 5. Sustainable living. 6. Climatic changes—Psychological aspects.
7. Climatic changes—Prevention. 8. Self-actualization (Psychology). I. Title.

GE56.S29A3 2015   333.72092   C2014-907657-6
                                                 C2014-907658-4

New Society Publishers' mission is to publish books that contribute in fundamental
ways to building an ecologically sustainable and just society, and to do so with the
least possible impact on the environment, in a manner that models this vision. We
are committed to doing this not just through education, but through action. The
interior pages of our bound books are printed on Forest Stewardship Council®-
registered acid-free paper that is 100% post-consumer recycled (100% old growth
forest-free), processed chlorine-free, and printed with vegetable-based, low-VOC
inks, with covers produced using FSC®-registered stock. New Society also works to
reduce its carbon footprint, and purchases carbon offsets based on an annual audit
to ensure a carbon neutral footprint. For further information, or to browse our
full list of books and purchase securely, visit our website at: www.newsociety.com

Nature may not be what it was, no,
but it isn't simply gone.
It's *waiting.*

— J. B. MacKinnon,
The Once and Future World

Contents

Acknowledgments

Rua Mercier, Karen Lee, Yaana Dancer, Carol Tulpar, Janie Brown, Lara Janze, Emily Rose, Lorraine Kidumae and my other colleagues from *The Writers Studio* at Simon Fraser University spent years helping me shape these stories. Their contributions were golden. *The Big Swim* feels like "our" book.

I learned much of what I needed to know about writing a book from my excellent mentor at *The Writers Studio*, Brian Payton, who also happens to be the author of one of my all-time favorite books, *Shadow of the Bear* and, most recently, *The Wind is Not a River*.

Amanda Pitre-Hayes, Anne Haven McDonell, Charlie Demers and Manda Aufochs Gillespie (aka The Green Mama who wrote *Giving Your Child a Healthy Start and a Greener Future*) gave me timely and very helpful advice on various chapters. So did Gerald Amos, Kathy Francis, Lorraine Hathaway and Erin Brown.

Linda Solomon, Founder and Editor-in-Chief of The Vancouver Observer, an award winning on-line news source, got me started writing a book. She gave me encouragement, practical support and generous friendship at every step along the way. Tzeporah Berman, author of *This Crazy Time*, took the manuscript under her expansive wings. Her belief in it came at a crucial moment and she generously helped push my book out into the world. Shaena Lambert, author of *Oh, My Darling*, provided guidance through the entire process, from encouraging me to enroll at *The Writers Studio* to giving the manuscript a brilliant substantive edit at just the right moment.

Those who know Barry Saxifrage might begin to imagine the support, love and intellect that he has brought to this endeavor through the years. Deena Chochinov held my hand through the scary parts and reminded me to celebrate the good ones.

I'm inspired by the people who are fully committed to seeking responsible government action on climate change. Kevin Washbrook of *Voters Taking Action on Climate Change* is one of many who spring to mind.

Last but not least, the scientists who provide a steady stream of climate research continually expand my understanding of my place in the world and how to inhabit it gratefully.

My heartfelt thanks goes to each of you.

CHAPTER ONE

The Big Swim

I PULL MYSELF THROUGH a tunnel of silk. The silk pushes on my skin, a light pressure surrounding my body. A billion microscopic bubbles burst against me and buoy me up. Suspended in water, I feel as though I am flying.

Swimmers refer to these sensations as the "water feel." It's the reason why people like me don't wear wet suits or even swimsuits. Although, for this swim, the Big Swim, I have made compromises. My swim partner, Chloe, her father, Noel, and I are swimming from Cortes Island to Quadra Island. They nestle in the inner sea between Vancouver Island and the mainland of British Columbia, five miles apart as the crow flies.

In June, we studied the 70-page tidal flow charts that show current strength and direction day-by-day and hour-by-hour. August 11 was the only favorable day when we were all available. Slack ebb tide was at 11:30 AM. We would be heading due west. If we started swimming at 8 AM, we should be able to avoid the strongest currents that endlessly sweep the inner coast waters north and south.

The water temperature is between 18 and 19 degrees Celsius. All summer I have worried about the cold of this swim. My solution is to cut off sleeves from a triathlon suit to protect my fatless arms, and a neoprene swim cap with a chin strap. I have covered my body with lanolin, the heavy golden oil from sheep's wool that looks and feels like ball-bearing grease. The net result of my helmet-like cap, shiny black arm warmers and glistening naked body is sublimely ridiculous. I look like a dominatrix who dropped her boots and crop into the sea and now has to dive in after them.

First comes the horrid moment of anticipation. Every day this summer, at six in the morning, I have met Chloe at the lake to share this moment. We know to get through it as quickly as possible, to throw our sleep-warm bodies into the chill without hesitation and kick as hard as we can, for heat as well as propulsion. Actually, I am far more aghast at the cold than Chloe. Any description of the perfect body type for open-water swimming describes Chloe: short and compact with well-distributed body fat. I am taller and pear-shaped. Generally I give my lower body an insulting regard, but when I'm swimming, I am grateful for the insulation. From waist to knee, I have never felt cold. As far as my slender upper body goes, Chloe and I swim in different seas. Mine are much, much colder.

Chloe's father, Noel, is a different creature altogether. His stroke is so swift and powerful, and his chest so expanded from deep breathing, that his upper body seems to glide slightly above the cold water.

I jump off the mother ship, an old-style fishing boat named the *Jenny Lynn*, into the sea and the shock of cold.

We've agreed we have to actually touch Cortes Island before swimming the five-mile channel to Quadra Island. In my moments of hesitation before jumping, Noel has already done this. He glides past in the opposite direction, sleek and regular as a mechanical seal. Chloe and I swim to the nearest rocky outcrop. I cut my fingers on some barnacles (surely this counts), and splash out toward Barry, my husband and guide, who waits in a yellow plastic kayak. He has done this for me before. He is a tech wizard and data lover who has the practical, tender qualities of a mother bird. I flail under his protective wing. He will do everything he can to keep me safe and, more relevantly, to minimize the distance from our starting point to our destination. I depend on him utterly. I am vulnerable and grateful.

After the silky, floating pressures of "water feel," the next best pleasure comes from the motion of swimming, the reach and pull of my arms. When I'm in the flow, the motion originates in my shoulders and my body sways from side to side with each stroke. It's a role reversal: usually my thick legs propel my weak upper body through mountain climbs, bike rides and even a marathon. Now my sleek, muscular arms and shoulders are doing the pulling. I'm so proud that they can rise to the occasion, after all those decades of being feeble.

Reach and pull—breathe, reach and pull—breathe, reach and pull—breathe. It's all I think about. Through repetition, I reach a state of grace, a zone of perfect moments, delicious movement and blessed water feel. If those perfect moments didn't possess me, I would despair at the infinitude of time and distance ahead.

The state of grace doesn't last forever. I pop my head up and look around. Marina Island lurks to the south. On the ferry ride, we don't come into the lee of Marina until close to the end. I realize I haven't gone very far.

"You're doing great!" my husband says. "What do you need?"

"Nothing. I'm just looking around."

The still, overcast day is perfect for the Big Swim. Gigantic clouds hover on distant islands, the sea shine reaches to the far away, rain slants down in grey columns. I'm a human pinprick in a vast rolling fabric. To be small, in open waters, away from humans' sawing and paving and spewing, returns to me my membership in something more beautiful and more infinitely complicated than humanity. The ocean is the biggest, most mysterious wilderness of all, and I'm in it.

There's a coast guard boat approaching. I squint through salt-riddled eyes. It's a scene from a magazine picture, two unbelievably handsome men and a beautiful woman in a huge orange Zodiac wearing big warm smiles and bright orange flotation suits.

"Is she okay?" one shouts, politely.

Barry knows how I feel about the ocean wilds, and he knows how I feel about motor craft. Already, I can smell a thin film of diesel on the water's surface. He will make them go away.

"She's doing great," he says.

It's clearly time to get swimming. I give the sea Mounties a jaunty thumbs-up, and plough back in.

Now there isn't much to say. It's cold, but not too cold. If I look up, I can see Chloe a bit behind me. Her parents-in-law are beside her in a skiff with an outboard motor. Noel is way ahead of me. I can't see him, but I can see his guide boat, a sleek blue kayak. Mostly, I'm just swimming. The states of grace arrive and disappear, swells of energy that lift and drop me, lift and drop me. In a state of grace, I'm fully aware of my most basic self. My spirit and my body are merged. When a state of grace fades, I'm left with my skinny arms and the cold pressing into my kidneys, going for my core.

When I next raise my head, my friend Meredith, who came along for the fun of kayaking, shouts, "You're two miles in by my chart!"

Distance reminders are a double-edged sword. I've done two miles. This is good, a major chunk, but I have three to go. I am less than halfway. This leads to all kinds of unhelpful inner calculations. Am I half spent? Am I getting colder? Can I do this? Why would I do this? What is the point of this?

This Big Swim business was not my idea. I am a come-along.

It began four years ago, when Chloe's husband, Tom, was working on our house. As Barry left for a soccer tournament, he gave me the news.

"Tom's leaving for the afternoon to go with Chloe and her dad on a Big Swim."

"Really?"

"From Mary Point to Sarah Point. You should go talk to him."

I found out they were swimming from Cortes Island to the mainland, about two miles. I hadn't trained, but I swam a lot. I was pretty sure this was for me, if they'd let me come with them.

They did let me come. My memories of that swim are blurred. I didn't have a boat to guide me, so I was looking up a lot to see where I was headed. The individual trees on the mainland were discernible from Cortes Island. Every time I looked up, I seemed to be almost there. Two hours of being "almost there" is unbearable. I left my body. It was like being in labor, a deep and ongoing pain made tolerable only by anticipation. But when I finally climbed out at Sarah Point, there was no baby to love. There was just me, with some part of my spirit gone missing. When I got home, I lay down on the sofa until it came back into me, with a nauseating jar.

I skipped the next year's Big Swim, two miles from Cortes to Hernando, but last year I trained with Chloe and we swam with her father to Mitlenatch Island, a wild islet four miles south of Cortes. It was a blustery day with the current and wind pushing us along. I felt like a flying fish, rising out of the swells for a few beats of the fin, then sinking back into the sea. It was gorgeous, and bitterly cold. The thought of the warm pebbled beach on Mitlenatch kept me going. When I finally crawled onto it, I burrowed into the warm stones. Barry covered my back with more warm stones. When I finally stood up again, the pebbles stuck to the lanolin I had used to coat my body. I was Pebble Woman, Aggregate Woman, Woman of the Tiny Rocks. The wardens of Mitlenatch came bustling over the hill from their cabin and stopped short. It took them a minute to formulate their questions. How did we get there? Why was I covered with pebbles? Would I be swimming back?

Chloe's father is the proximate cause of the Big Swims. He is a small, quiet man who is the architect of large public buildings, like airports and museums. He swims in the ocean year-round in Vancouver. These are his Big Swims. Chloe and I come along. Chloe comes along sturdily, capably, matter-of-factly, spreading the word around the island so that, when the day of the Big Swim arrives, everyone I see is wishing me good luck. I could never spread our aspirations so widely. I appreciate Chloe's good health in this regard and bask in the attention it brings me.

If Chloe's father is the proximate cause, what are the deeper causes of the Big Swim for me? Why, in the words I chattered out to Barry about halfway between islands, do I do this, when it is so damn cold? Maybe the answer is the same as Chloe's: it's a patrimony.

I remember Massachusetts, 1966, the Boston Marathon, Heartbreak Hill. There's a stout, short man with a comb-over and burly legs chugging up. He'd be faster walking, but he's somehow making the distance longer with an effortful jog. The rain is turning to sleet. I'm seven, in a beige fake-fur coat and red polyester mittens connected by elastic through my sleeves. We've been standing in the cold for hours, my brother pulling my mittens as far as he can and snapping them back at me. I'm near tears. My mother is wearing nylons, low-heeled pumps and a black sweater dress with a sewn-in vest of bright primary stripes. Her hair is stacked up, her makeup tasteful, a lovely woman in a genteel, amusing world. But she's cold too.

My father jogs up to where we are waiting by the side of

road to cheer him on. I barely recognize him. I'm used to the well-dressed man who exudes certainty regarding the topography of this world and the one beyond. But now he looks awful. White spittle clings to his blue lips. He exhales in explosive puffs, blue terry-cloth headband askew. His silver metallic liner gloves remind me of Mickey Mouse. But he's in a tunnel of determination. Will he even see us?

We shout "Hey, Dad!" and cheer him on. He glances up, then down, as though he is unable to acknowledge us due to pain. Then he mutters from the side of his mouth, "Get me some hooch."

What?

My brother runs beside him.

"What did you say, Dad?"

"*Get-me-some-hooch,*" he spits out, irritated at the precious effort wastefully expended in repeating his request.

My brother runs back to my mom.

"Dad says he wants hooch," he says, mystified.

"What's hooch?" I ask.

"Alcohol," my mom says, carefully neutral.

We stand there in the sleet, stunned. I have never seen my father drink alcohol, ever. He's a family doctor, a church elder, an example on a pedestal. There's no drinking up there, ever.

We get the hooch and find him again. He tips back the Dixie cup of vodka proffered by my mom without a blink or sputter.

"More," he rasps. This time he sloshes it around his mouth then spits it out onto the asphalt. Mom winces. He survives the marathon but loses his toenails. I am left with my childhood confusion as to why he does this horrible thing every single year.

My conscious lesson from this and other similar childhood experiences is to reject my father's tunnel-like determination in favor of *joie de vivre*. If I'm not experiencing pleasure, I'm not doing it. Painful acts of endurance just seem pointless.

On the other hand, maybe my swimming comes from a genetic pull. My father engaged the world's great places with his arduous goals. He water-skied the Volga River in Russia. He ran the route from Marathon to Athens and finished with a triumphant sprint up the Acropolis in shorts that looked like underwear, holding a Sterno can spray-painted gold on a torch while we hid behind pillars. I followed in his footsteps up the Matterhorn. He claimed to do these things for glory, but that explanation never seemed sufficient.

Anyway, I have nothing to prove. For the Big Swim, the balance of sensation is toward pleasure. The water feel, the swim dance, the wild sea, these outweigh the sensation of cold. Yet the question persists: what am I doing out here so far from land?

Sometimes I pull myself through the water fuelled by an anxiety that is as distinct as an outboard motor. It is a dark and desperate force, a combination of untied ends and misspoken words, the sum of my malfeasance in life churning through my body. In the ocean, it all slips away. I'm a devil shedding evil in the cool, bubbly waters.

Romantically speaking, I'm part ocean mammal. I spend time thinking about how real mermaids would actually swim. What if it's more like a fish than a whale? I can actually feel where my human body tapers to a point at my groin and my dolphin body begins. Sometimes I hold my legs tight together and beat through the water as they do. Whales would greet me if they met me and let me ride a fin. In eye contact with dolphins and seals, I've seen my own curiosity reflected there. I'm strongly related to the marine branch of the family tree.

In one of my first memories, I'm four and swimming in a mudhole someone dug for me and my best friend. At five, I dog paddled with my face to the sky and my arms and legs vertically churning me across the public pool while my older sisters and brothers cheered me on, because our parents had promised a backyard pool once we could all swim a lap. I spent so much time in that pool that my white-blond hair was mossy green. At the beach, I shrieked as my dad catapulted me from his shoulders into the waves, another memory dazzled by sparkling droplets.

Meanwhile, I'm still swimming, somewhere way out in the middle, miles from land in any direction. The sea shines a duller grey as dark clouds approach. Bubbles trail from my fingertips.

When I raise my head the next time, fat drops are plopping all around me. Upside-down teardrops arise from hundreds of tiny, yet expanding circles. The rain makes a small chirping sound.

"Cricket rain," Barry says.

It's the title of a friend's poem. Barry wears neoprene, wet yet warm, attentive yet bored. I find his warm brown eyes through the blur of rain. We smile. I put my head down again.

When I breathe to the left, I see the open strait to the south. When I breathe to the right, I see Barry in the cheery yellow kayak, always about three feet ahead. He never seems to paddle. I must be going really slowly. This negative thought leads me downward. The cold is seeping deeper into me. My peripheral circulation has shut down. My hands, I know, are white. Blood may be struggling to get to my vital organs. Cold is pain. This cold has reached an inescapable level. I tolerate. Then I endure. And I still find those states of grace, the sheath of muscles from spine to shoulder deliciously stretching out as I reach beyond my head, pushing my hands through the water past my torso, finishing the arc of my arms with a final thrust. I enjoy the pleasurable hold of the silky sea. The cold is a fact I can cope with. I swim on and on.

When I lift my head, I can see the bright beige band of Quadra Island's low-tide beach.

"You're doing great!" Meredith yells, waving her paddle. "You're almost there!"

Barry remains knowingly silent. We have covered the sensitivities of "almost there" in other swims because, in my experience, being almost there is by far the worst part. When you are almost there, swimming is all about dragging yourself to the destination. Distance viewed from the water is deceptive, and the shore is still at least thirty minutes away. There is no access to timeless grace. Time and distance, now finite, become intolerable. The cold boldly pierces. Muscles tweak and twinge.

I lift my head to the trusty yellow kayak and ask Barry for a mask and snorkel. Perhaps I will see other life to distract me, to help me with the time ahead. In these seas, I have watched the luminous domes of moon jellies floating past like UFOs through empty space. Lion's mane jellyfish with shock-inducing stings have floated well beneath me, thick rust-red ruffles trailing from their flowery bodies. I've glimpsed deep silver flashes of salmon, schools of small round-bellied perch and even a foot-long squid whose eye focused on me with deep regard. I've thrown myself in with the roiling black-and-white bodies of Pacific white-sided dolphins, surrounded by the rasping gurgles of dolphin breath, breathing in their steam.

Here there is nothing. Dark green fades into dark brown. Not even a jellyfish floats by. I am alone in a huge, empty, very cold room.

I begin to watch for the bottom to rise from the depths and change the water hues. But there's nothing, nothing, nothing, minutes and minutes and minutes of nothing. I lift my head. The beach appears the same distance away. Barry and Meredith hover. The coast guard boat has returned to the vicinity. Our mother ship, the crisp blue-and-white *Jenny Lynn*, is anchored up ahead. I put my head down and sputter on. I am thoroughly spent. For the first time, the strokes are an act of mind over body. I am not dancing. I am marching, forcing myself, wanting it to end. I am willing, after all, to enter my father's tunnel of determination. Maybe it goes back beyond him. My doggedness, his doggedness, expresses even older genes. Pioneer women with tight mouths who wear lacy collars and big skirts cheer me on. It's another state of grace. It builds and ebbs.

Then, finally, the hues change. Dark blobs take shape. Fluid seaweed forms become discernible and brighten until I am above radiant gardens of green, orange, red, yellow, purple, gold and crimson. Brilliant fronds wave beneath me. It is the brightest, most beautiful seaweed I have ever seen. I drift for a moment, soaking in the colors and the fact that I have swum along the ferry route from Cortes to Quadra Island.

I crawl onto the shore, too cold and watery to walk. Everyone cheers; Barry, Meredith, the coast guard and our friends aboard the *Jenny Lynn*. I sit on the seaweed-covered stones and watch Chloe in the last few minutes of her swim. We cheer again as she stumbles onto shore. She looks terrible, her eyes bloodshot, her face swollen, the coat of lanolin turned white, flecks of seaweed clinging to her naked body.

We climb aboard Chloe's guide boat, which takes us to the *Jenny Lynn*. Noel is standing on the deck, arms folded, wrapped in a pale red blanket. He finished his swim an hour ago and looks warm and dignified. The coast guard boat is tied abreast. As we climb aboard, the children gape at us with big eyes. In fact, everyone looks slightly shocked by our appearance. I realize that I must look as bad as Chloe, or worse.

I need help to get aboard. My friend Laura seats me, and one of the coast guard officers sticks two giant warm packs behind my back. I cling to Laura for warmth. She holds me with the physical expertise of a nursing mother.

A coast guard officer appears with a breathing mask. I obediently put it to my mouth, thinking I must be really sick. He explains that the heated air will help me warm up, but the heated air smells stale. It brings me to my senses. I don't need this stuff. I thank him, hand it back and suck the fresh sea air. Tom hands me a bottle of Glenlivet, which I gratefully accept. The officer scowls.

"You looked just like an ocean baby being born," Laura's mother tells me, "all green and blue coming over the gunwale. That lanolin looked like vernix, and you were covered with seaweed. It's a sight I'll never forget."

This reminds me of my ridiculous swim helmet and sleeves. I am recovered enough to become self-conscious and remove them quickly.

The Big Swim is over. It took three hours and forty minutes. There is more Scotch to be drunk, a deep sleep to be had, a celebratory dinner out, a night of dancing at the hall with friends hugging and congratulating me. In retrospect, I think of the Big Swim as an exclamation mark, punctuating the summer.

And I might even understand why I do it. Big Swims make me feel as though I'm part water creature with cool skin and damp hair, fed by elements and ecosystems, creeks and springs. I belong, temporarily, to a vast, cold world where brilliant seaweed banners wave in exultation.

For moments on end, I am a perfect creature. And it is such a beautiful world.

CHAPTER TWO

Pumpkin People

I'VE WANTED CONTROL over my own food production ever since I learned at the age of eight that you're supposed to wash apples, not because of bug poo, but because of poisonous pesticides. I also suffered from a vague form of survivalist's discomfort, a sense of accelerating toward a wall along a path that people loosely referred to as "unsustainability." The Smith and Hawken's gardening catalog played a role with its depiction of the wholesomely elegant foodie digging with her hand-forged English garden fork, just a bit of dirt under her nails. Barry and I explained to family and friends that our organic homestead would allow us to grow food with vastly better flavor and nourishment.

We had created gardens at every house we had ever rented but had no experience in larger-scale food production. So when I wrapped up my legal work in Seattle before Barry wrapped up his tech work, I applied to the Linnaea Farm Organic Gardening Programme on Cortes Island. The application charmed me with such questions as "What is your favorite vegetable and why?"

"Among many beautiful and delicious vegetables," I wrote, "few grow to stupendous size. For this, I admire the pumpkin most of all."

I could have gone on about its celebrity status in children's literature: Linus's Great Pumpkin who rewards sincerity, an under sung virtue; or Cinderella's sparkly pumpkin carriage drawn by four white horses. What girl doesn't want a ride in that coach? Or Peter Peter Pumpkin Eater, who had a wife and couldn't keep her. In retrospect, what a creep. But he did manage to grow a pumpkin big enough to hold an adult. I couldn't even grow a pumpkin that would fit my two-year-old niece, although I came pretty close. Instead I carved it into a huge jack-o'-lantern, an admirably ubiquitous folk art.

The pumpkin I grew during organic gardening school weighted well over 100 pounds. Someone suggested that I present it to the Pumpkin People who competed each year to grow the biggest pumpkin on the island. Although I didn't follow through, I expected that these people, the Pumpkin People, would someday be my people.

Gary was the first Pumpkin Person I met. He has always lived on Cortes and rarely leaves. He fishes, digs clams, hunts, gathers and then brings his abundance to his friends with a big, easy smile and clear blue eyes. He explained to me that someone named Serge gave him a pumpkin seedling every spring. Serge started all the seeds on the exact same day under the exact same conditions so that all the contestants would be at the same starting line. Then he delivered them to the other Pumpkin People and let them select their seedling on the same day.

After that, the race was on. All season long, the Pumpkin People urged their seedlings with ingredients that tended to favor those who did manual labor in the sea or on farms, such as seaweed, the starfish that oyster farmers cleaned off their rafts and various kinds of animal manure. In the fall, according to Gary, the pumpkins were ceremonially weighed by Serge, who drove around in his truck with a giant scale. Then the contestants had a victory feast of food from the forest, sea and garden.

For three years straight, I asked Gary if I could have a seedling.

"Sure," he'd say. "I'll talk to Serge."

But even with Gary's help, I never made it onto Serge's list. It gradually dawned on me that it might have to do with my role as a director of the Cortes Ecoforestry Society, which opposed industrial logging on the island's Crown and timber company lands. Our success meant that tree fellers like Serge had small jobs or had to go off-island to work. Still, I felt the arena of big vegetables should be a meritocracy, unsullied by politics. In a former life, I had competed with reasonable success: good schools, academic scholarships and interesting jobs. As an islander, I danced like a heathen at parties and, like the other Pumpkin People, spent a huge amount of my time in the garden. How could I be disallowed from the pumpkin in-crowd? They were romantic and fascinating. I wanted in.

One year, at Gary's recommendation, we hired Serge to fell some big hemlocks next to our house. Serge has a rosy round face with bright, quick eyes. He is not so tall, with a curly beard and a ponytail. The day he felled our trees, he wore a grey wool undershirt stretched over his firm, round belly.

"When I am working for the timber companies," he told me, "I ride from one big clear-cut to another in the bucket of a helicopter with my chain saw. The cut blocks are so large; it is too far to walk."

After he had landed the hemlocks with surgical precision, I asked him for a big pumpkin seedling.

"Yes, Gary said you wanted this," he said with a roguish smile, "I will see what I can do."

I waited for that seedling all spring. We cleared the garden beds, started transplants in the greenhouse and planted peas. We ate rich, green nettles from an abandoned homestead cooked with eggs and feta cheese. Orange and red salmonberries from the roadside satisfied our winter hunger for bright fruit. As spring progressed, the alders along the driveway turned misty red with new buds, and the blackberry vines sprouted shoots of pure green vigor. We transplanted broccoli, lettuce and onions. But Serge never delivered a pumpkin seedling. When I saw Gary at a potluck in the early summer, he showed polite surprise that Serge hadn't included me.

"He must have forgotten," Gary said. "My pumpkin plant is growing really well this year."

After his pumpkin won, he showed me the certificate he received, a 5 × 7 card hand-painted by a Pumpkin Person artist: a beautiful orange pumpkin on a vibrant blue background. A banner stretched above the pumpkin with Gary's name, the weight of his pumpkin and the year. Gary described the chanterelle pie someone had brought to the feast. I realized the truth that he was too kind to state: I would never be invited into the Pumpkin People, regardless of my shared passion for enormous vegetables. I would have to prove myself, in some incontrovertible manner.

The next winter, I went online to order seeds from big pumpkins.com and, while I was at it, a book on how to grow huge pumpkins. For weeks, I put the manure from our pet horse Goldie in a pile on the driveway, near the hose for easy watering.

In early June, Gary dropped off his daughter to play with my son and mentioned that he had transplanted his seedling from Serge outside. As the children ran down to the strawberry bed, I took him to the greenhouse to see my seedling. The leaves were the size of dessert plates. After Gary left, I transplanted it into the six-foot pile of manure. I patted down a hollow at the base of the vine, so water would soak in.

In late June, when the sugar snap peas were the size of my ring finger, I placed the hose in the hollow and turned it on as I hiked down the hill to pick peas. A half hour later, when I returned with my big metal bowl full of sweet, crunchy sugar snaps, I turned the hose off again. By the time the sprouting broccoli waved its hundred purple scepters throughout the garden, the pumpkin had 15 leaves the size of dinner plates.

Gary came tromping up the drive in his gumboots with a bucket of prawns. I watched him through the kitchen window as he stopped in front of the pumpkin plant and stared.

"That's a big pumpkin plant," he said when he came in the door. "It's bigger than any of Serge's."

I smiled and offered him snap peas from the bowl.

The next day, I noticed the alder leaves were big enough to sway and rustle in the cool breeze. I buried the prawn shells in the pumpkin manure pile on my way to the lower garden to transplant a confetti of lettuce starts: green and red colors, smooth and frilly textures. On the way back up to the house, I noticed the big pumpkin had opened its first yellow flower to show an orange waxy pistil inside.

All through July, I knelt in the sawdust path and peeked under the leaves of the raspberry bushes. We nudged the berries off their cores into the yogurt containers that hung from our necks with orange baling twine. By that time, the big pumpkin plant had runners that I had to train along the side of the driveway to keep it clear, and several pale yellow fruits.

In late July, the yellow plums came ripe and squirted sweet water when we bit into the taut, tart skins. By then, two of the baby pumpkins had rotted, but the third one was swelling up. The pumpkin leaves were so rampant that I couldn't get to the base of the plant without stepping on them. I tiptoed through them and plunged a 4-inch PVC pipe into the manure pile. I stuck the hose in the pipe and kept a trickle of water running into the mound toward the roots.

My mom came to visit. When I picked her up from the float plane, she wore all white, like the yachties who cruise into Cortes Bay on boats worth ten times the amount of a Cortes homestead. I had lost track of time weeding the garden and hadn't changed from my baggy, stained, long-sleeved shirt and ripped canvas pants. I dragged her crisp red rolling suitcase down the dusty driveway lined with alders and blackberries. She stopped at the giant pumpkin plant and stared.

"Now, tell me what's going on here," she said.

I explained about the tightly knit Pumpkin People and my attempt to break in with a huge pumpkin. She stared silently at the lumpy mass. Perhaps she was thinking about all those university tuition bills she had paid. Then she said, "Well, aren't you clever," and walked on.

For the first two weeks of August, we ate entire dinners of green beans, sometimes steamed and drizzled with garlic butter, sometimes sautéed in hot chili oil with tofu or sausage. I cooked the first zucchini in butter until it was mellow and sweet. When we passed through the greenhouse, we stripped Concord grapes from their clusters for a sweet-tart mouthful. Meanwhile, the pumpkin grew. When Gary came to dinner with his family, he looked it over and shook his head.

One day in August, the angle of the beach-ball-sized pumpkin seemed different. I waded through the sea of leaves and looked down at the base of the vine: the weight of the pumpkin had snapped it. I felt sick. My outsized ambition to be a Pumpkin Person had required all the time and nutrients I had to spare. If this pumpkin died, I would never be able to match my level of effort again, and I would never be a Pumpkin Person.

I knelt down to view the damage. The vine still held with fibers along the bottom. I walked up to the house and found the pumpkin-growing book in a stack of seed catalogs. It stated that some growers intentionally pierce the vine to their largest pumpkin so that they can wick nutrients directly to it. The book advised using milk. No way. I had already used too much of our horse manure for an essentially ornamental purpose.

Instead, I made compost tea from comfrey and chicken manure in a plastic bucket and put a piece of string from the bucket into the broken pumpkin vine to create a nutrient wick. I threw a handful of weeds or a spade full of horse manure into the compost tea bucket when I passed by each morning on my way to fill my basket with our small, dense orange-red peaches that we ate with blackberries on our porridge.

The pumpkin swelled like a water balloon. By the time we dug the potatoes in late August, I could see the pale orange blob from the deck as I shucked the starchy Indian corn that we prefer.

In early September, the Irish Peach apples came ripe. We plowed tortilla chips into big bowls full of home-grown tomatoes, cilantro, garlic and onions. The pumpkin got bigger and uglier. One day, as I sat on the deck and wove the tops of storage onions around baling twine to hang in the root cellar, I heard a truck pull in at the gate. Gary walked up the drive with some cartons full of eggs from the world's happiest hens. He stopped at the pumpkin plant and stared. He scratched his head.

When he reached the deck, he said, "That's the biggest pumpkin I've ever seen. Serge says he wants to have a look."

"He's welcome to stop by," I said.

In late September, I had to step around the pumpkin vines to climb the plum tree. I squeezed my bare feet into the crooks of branches and reached for the pendulous fruit. I made plum cake with caramelized brown sugar at the bottom of the pan. We found the first chanterelles in the forest and the Prince mushroom in a hollow near the beach for wild mushroom pie.

Gary came back with a boatload of sockeye salmon so we went to the public dock with garbage bags and bought enough for the year. We cut the fish into fillets and steaks on the big stone table in the yard while the wasps flew around our hands. The fish broth from the heads became stock for paella with clams we dug from the lagoon. I dumped some boiled fish heads in the pumpkin's compost tea and returned the bones and clam shells to the sea. We bought half a lamb from a friend. The freezer was stuffed with fish, meat, raspberries and peaches.

We admired our beautiful Bartlett pears and sautéed pear slices in butter. We walked around the orchard and tasted the fruit from our young trees: flavor of almonds in one, the scent of perfume in another. Their names filled our tongues: Gravenstein Teal Crimson, Orenco, Chisel Jersey, Aromatic Russet.

Barry climbed the chestnut trees out back and shook them. We sat on the deck in leather gloves and pulled the shiny brown nuts from their spine cases with forks. I lay in the afternoon sun to read a romance novel and eat a bowl of apples.

It rained, and the pumpkin swelled to almost the size of an easy chair. We set the winter squash on boards in the field to keep them off the wet soil while their skins hardened. Beans dried on a sheet on the greenhouse floor. In the evenings, we shelled and sorted them by color: black, white, red, gold and speckled.

We fed apple mash into the old-style Italian grape press that went crk CRK crk CRK as the gear pressed down the wooden slabs that squeezed the mash. We put canning jars under the spout of the press and drank sun-sugared sweetness.

In early-October, we collected more wild mushrooms. The boletes showed up at the foot of ferny cliffs, and pine mushrooms humped up the moss beside old Douglas firs. The kids made forts in the trees while the adults rambled by with baskets. After a windstorm, we drove the truck to the shore, placed a plank as a ramp, and wheelbarrowed seaweed from the windrows piled up on the cobble beach. Serge was there with his big white diesel truck.

"This seaweed is very good for pumpkins," he said. "Gary tells me you have a big pumpkin."

"Yes, I do," I said.

"I would like to see this pumpkin."

"Come by any time."

"I will come with my scale to weigh it."

"Good," I said. "It is very ugly."

"That is what Gary told me," Serge said.

When I got home, I put a handful of seaweed in the compost tea. The rest we laid on the garden beds. A few days later, I covered the seaweed with alder leaves raked from a road behind our house. I heard Serge's diesel truck drive up to the gate and went to meet him.

Serge jumped out of the cab with a friend. He looked at my gigantic, misshapen pumpkin and whistled.

"She's a big one," he said, "but ugly."

He sent me off to find plywood so that he could roll the pumpkin on to the scale. He took the big digital scale out of his truck bed. The three of us strained to roll the huge pumpkin up the plywood on to the scale. Nothing registered. We rolled it back down.

Serge stepped on to the scale to test it: 198 pounds.

"I am not too fat," he commented, "I am just too short. I'm supposed to be six foot six."

We rolled the pumpkin back up the ramp. No read out. We rolled the pumpkin off. Serge's friend climbed on: 178 pounds.

"Yes, the scale, it works," said Serge.

We rolled the pumpkin back on, slowly, and watched as it went up to 298 pounds and then blinked off.

"It is too big for the scale!" Serge exclaimed. "The scale stops at three hundred pounds. Your pumpkin weighs more than three hundred pounds!"

He shook his head, truly impressed. "My biggest pumpkin was 276 pounds," he said. "You have won for sure."

He gave me a congratulatory hug and kiss. A zing passed from his soft red lips onto mine. We exchanged a startled glance.

"Maybe people will pay to guess the weight, and the money will go to the new medical clinic," Serge said as he gazed across the field. "The medical clinic is not political."

"Everyone needs health care," I agreed looking at the garden, some beds full of kale and leeks and others covered with leaves.

"The deer like the pumpkin meat, so do the sheep," Serge said. "You can put your pumpkin in the bush after we weigh it. I will call you tomorrow about the winner's banquet, maybe hot dogs at Smelt Bay."

That night, we ate dinner at the house of our friends Jane and Raphael. Jane is tall and quiet. Raphael pulls people into his streams of enthusiasm. They had butchered three lambs earlier that day, and we cooked little pieces of fresh organ meat in fondue pots full of water with thyme: heart, kidney, liver and lung. For dessert, Jane served a thin white cake rolled up with raspberries and cream. As she cut into it, the phone rang. Serge had tracked me down.

"There is *another* pumpkin that tops the scale," he said. He sounded very happy. "I don't know if you have won. Marc's pumpkin is too big for the scale."

"It is a good looking pumpkin," he added. "It is in the community hall if you want to see it. Bring a flashlight to shine through the window."

"I will bring my pumpkin to the community hall so we can compare them side by side," I said.

"Your pumpkin is too big to move," Serge said.

"How did Marc's pumpkin get to the community hall?"

"We rolled it up a ramp," Serge said.

We sat around Jane and Raphael's dinner table and analyzed the situation. It didn't look good.

Marc, like Serge, is French Canadian. He had lived on the island a long time. I was an American. I had lived on the island for as long as Marc. I had been a Canadian citizen for years, but that could never change the facts. I was an American.

Marc had used a proper Pumpkin Person seedling, saved from a previous year's winner and hand-delivered to him by Serge. I had ordered mine online from bigpumpkins.com.

Marc did manual work. I did manual work as well, but I had once practiced law in the US which made me a lawyer and, of course, an American.

Marc didn't serve on any community boards that I knew of, and he was generous within the community, like Serge. I was a director of the Ecoforestry Society, which was very political. My husband and I were generous with community environmental efforts, and this too was political.

Marc presumably fed his pumpkin with seaweed, fish guts and starfish, in the same manner that Serge and Gary and all the other Pumpkin People fed theirs. I fed my pumpkin with the manure of a pet horse and wicked compost tea into the vine, as suggested in a book.

Last but not least, Marc went to last year's Halloween dance dressed as Serge. He grew a short, curly beard for the occasion and wore a tight sweater over a fake belly. He beamed, winked and waved. He won first prize. I went as a tree.

We decided that, given the facts, I had to get my pumpkin to the hall for a side-by-side comparison. In the heat of our search for justice, we decided to go get my pumpkin then and there. But it was dark and cold outside.

"We'll do it tomorrow," Raphael said. "The hall is locked at night."

My family drove by the hall on the way home and shone a headlamp through the window. There was Marc's pumpkin, big, round and orange. I lifted my six-year-old son up so he could see it too.

"Sweet pumpkin," he said.

The next day, I found Raphael and some other friends at a sustainability fair at the hall. We went to get my pumpkin. I parked my old green truck next to the vine on the drive and found a fish net in the barn. We rolled the pumpkin onto the net and, to Raphael's count, strained to lift it up into the truck bed. The fish net bulged, but held. I drove slowly back to the hall where people moved aside to make room for our fish net stretcher bearing the pale, slumping hulk. We set it down next to Marc's firm, round, bright orange pumpkin. My pumpkin looked like a GMO monster that could attack his pretty vegetable. Around me, people murmured how ugly it was.

"You're proud of it, I can tell," a friend accused me.

"No. I am embarrassed," I said. "If any factor other than weight and size can be considered in the contest, it will lose. It should lose. All I want is a seedling next year."

"It is a weight and size contest," my friend pointed out. "Yours will win."

I gave a resigned shrug, then felt a smile creep across my face.

The next day, I filled my truck with gas at Squirrel Cove, and Serge drove up in his big white truck.

"Did you see my pumpkin at the hall?" I asked.

"Yes, I saw it," he said. "We are going to use the pumpkins

to raise money for the health clinic. People will pay to guess which weighs more."

I waited.

"The health clinic is not political," he reminded me with a smile. "Then we will have hot dogs at Smelt Bay."

"That sounds good," I said.

"We will have to cut the pumpkins up to weigh them," Serge said. "They probably lose about 25 pounds a week inside the hall. They are drying out."

The next weekend Jane, Raphael, Barry and I went camping on a nearby island. The pumpkins still had not been weighed. As we walked through the deep forest, we talked about how the big pumpkin contest rules could be bent to favor a certain contestant. They could use a chain saw to cut the pumpkins up for weighing and move the saw around more in one pumpkin than another so that it would lose more weight in the cut. They could wait to weigh them because a larger pumpkin had a greater surface area and would dehydrate more quickly.

When we got home from camping, there was a message from Serge on the answering machine.

"It is about the big pumpkin," he said. "It is leaking in the hall and rotting onto the floor. They want it out of there. We have to cut it up and weigh it very soon. By the way, we made $207 for the health clinic. Call me to talk about the pumpkin."

I called him, and we decided to meet at the hall the next day to cut my pumpkin up and weigh it.

"I will have to use a chain saw," Serge said.

My sister, a geology professor, called that night. She had just made a big round soccer ball costume for her daughter for Halloween, and she felt very proud.

"My whole life has been preparing me for this," she said. "The home economics courses, the science of crystalline structures."

I told her about Serge and my big pumpkin. We paid trib-
ute to the seminal influence of a big round pumpkin costume
our mom had made for our brother long ago. Perhaps it inspired both my big pumpkin growing obsession and my sister's
soccer ball costume that, if orange, would be a pumpkin.

"I think your whole life has been preparing you for this big
pumpkin contest," she said. "The gardening, the lawyering."

"The pumpkin is disgustingly ugly," I replied, "but I will do
my best to have it fairly weighed."

"Be careful," she cautioned. "These things can start a grudge
that lasts generations."

Then Raphael called and offered to come to the hall the
next morning in case I needed help.

The next morning, I packed up towels, two kitchen knives
and a digital camera. Serge had a wheelbarrow, a shovel, a
pruning saw and a carpenter's saw. No chain saw.

My ugly pumpkin had leaked beige goo on the hall floor.
It also had big dark spots of rot all over it. We hoped that we
could get it out of the hall without it collapsing. Two respected
gardeners, Frank and Peggy, showed up with a clipboard. It
was a mail day, and a lot of people walked by. They shook their
heads, some in wonderment, most in disgust.

"I heard she force fed it," someone whispered.

"That's no pumpkin," someone else said. "That's a squash."

This was true. Bigpumpkins.com in fact sells Atlantic Giant
squashes, which resemble, but are not, true pumpkins.

Frank took a picture of Serge and me by the pumpkin, smiling with our arms around each other.

"Lucky you brought it to the hall early," Serge commented.
"We generally don't accept rotting pumpkins."

Then he drove home for a piece of plastic to roll the pumpkin on to, to contain the mess.

Once we got the pumpkin on to the plastic, we skooched it outside. The pumpkin held. I cleaned up the trail of beige liquid with a mop from the janitor's closet. By the time I came outside, Serge had sawed several chunks out of the pumpkin. Inside was a sea of orange-brown goop and big seeds. Frank scooped some seeds into a cup to plant the next year.

"I don't think we should weigh the liquid," said Serge. "Just the pumpkin meat."

"The liquid is inside the pumpkin," I protested. "If we hadn't cut it open, it would count."

"But how do we weigh it?" Serge asked.

Peggy took a trash can from the hall and emptied it. After weighing the trash can, we scooped the goop into it, first with a small bucket and then with the shovel, and weighed it again. Serge sawed off chunks of pumpkin, and we weighed those. Peggy wrote down the weight of each piece. Raphael arrived and grinned, his hands in his pockets. People stopped to observe.

"A classic Cortes moment," someone commented, as Serge hacked at the remaining pumpkin mess with his shovel.

When it was over, Peggy added up the chunk and liquid weights: 312.7 pounds.

"We'd better weigh Marc's too," Frank said. "It has brown spots on it. It might not last much longer."

"The scale won't weigh it," Serge said. "And I cannot cut up the pumpkin without Marc here."

"Let's try it whole," said Frank. "It looks smaller."

We rolled Marc's pumpkin onto the scale: 212.4 pounds. Serge shook his head in amazement.

"I don't understand it," he said. "The last time, it broke the scale."

Raphael winked at me.

We wheeled the gooey innards of my pumpkin into the alder grove behind the hall for the deer. The chunks went into Frank's truck for his sheep.

"They are used to better food, I think," Serge observed. "I will call you about the victory party. I think we will enjoy our hot dogs," he said. He winked at me as we left the hall.

We didn't eat hot dogs at Smelt Bay. Serge rented the hall for the best feast I had ever attended: wild venison, sockeye salmon, apple juice, winter squash, apple pie, potatoes, chanterelles and every other good thing that can be found on the island in late October. I brought a salad of chopped kale with feta cheese, dried cranberries, toasted walnuts and a garlicky balsamic vinaigrette dressing. I spent my prize money on a bottle of Scotch and found a tugboat captain who reminded me of my oldest brother to share it with. I reminded him of his wife's sister, and before long, we felt like family. The rest of the money went to the health center. I received a beautiful hand-painted certificate with the year and the weight of the pumpkin.

I had a speech prepared that acknowledged the different seed source, the unorthodox wick method of fertilization, the terrible appearance of my pumpkin and the way it leaked on the hall floor. The speech ended with a formal request for a Pumpkin Person seedling. But the Pumpkin People's feast was rowdy and informal, and for a moment, I recognized something overweening in my intense desire to belong there. Instead, we toasted big pumpkins.

Serge asked me to order him seeds from bigpumpkin.com, so I did. The next spring, as I tugged at rotting stumps of kale that were as thick as my wrists, I heard his diesel truck come down our lane. It turned left at the Y, into our neighbor's driveway. I stopped working and listened to them talk about pumpkin seedlings. Then the truck door slammed and the engine started. I stood, feet in the mud, waiting. Sure enough, the truck turned at the Y and headed up our drive. I threw down my gloves and ran up to the gate to meet Serge and receive my pumpkin seedling. Every year since then, we have grown Atlantic Giant squashes, not pumpkins, and I have not won, but I have feasted.

CHAPTER THREE

Hare

A<small>T TIMES</small> the 1,000 people who live year-round on Cortes Island seem to divide into two camps: redneck and tree hugger. So I was surprised when Lisa McKenzie approached me at a community hall dinner. Her family had helped settle Cortes Island and still earned its living from logging. I had emigrated from the United States where I practiced environmental law. We had kids near the same age, but hers were at the public school and my son was at Linnaea, the alternative school with a nature-based curriculum. As Lisa caught my eye and made her way across the room, I couldn't think of what she might have to say to me. She looked so cute in her hand-embroidered sweater and tight jeans, her brown hair and freckles. I smiled at her.

"I had an epiphany this week," she said. "I was unhappy so I drew up a big bubble bath and lit the candles all around me. I was lying in the tub, wondering what was wrong with me. Then it struck me. I'm not having enough fun."

She paused. I nodded.

"So I want to be in your group of friends."

The words "Even though you are environmentalists," hung unspoken in the air.

"You guys look like you're having fun, and I want to have more fun too."

She finished by spreading her arms out and leaning back on one leg, "Tah dah!"

"That sounds good," I said.

We hugged like sisters from a different life.

After that night, our group included Lisa. We hiked through the forest all over the island and danced every time a band played at the community hall. Our families hunted chanterelles in the fall, rented a ski condo in the winter and camped in the summer. Lisa got a job as a teacher's assistant at Linnaea. As the school's business administrator, I saw how she could teach kids anything—math, line dancing, conflict resolution, driftwood art, you name it. Lisa enrolled her daughter and son at the school.

But it wasn't easy for her to have environmentalist friends and a logger family. The two groups had strong disagreements about the island forests, which were mostly 80-year-old cedars and Douglas firs with some patches of old-growth. Everyone wanted to see forest jobs as part of the island economy, but the environmentalists advocated logging so slowly that, to the loggers, the whole island might as well be a park.

Lisa's father was prominent in the social group of the loggers, which centered around the Volunteer Fire Department. James could fell a tree spot on its intended mark. He served on the board of the Ecoforestry Society, which was committed to slow, sustainable forestry, until he realized just how slow logging could become.

Lisa's mother, Becky McKenzie, had raised five kids. She also hunted, gardened and painted. Lisa snuck me in to her parents' house once to show me Becky's painting of a sockeye salmon run on the floor next to the stove, lifelike, finely detailed and full of admiration for the fish. She was the kind of woman I hoped I would have become if I'd grown up on the island: capable, tough and creative.

But as it happened, our politics were quite different. Lisa told me her mom thought the island was being overrun by environmentalists, thanks to the Hollyhock Lifelong Learning Centre. Hollyhock is a gorgeous relaxation and educational retreat on the beach near the south end of the island. People attend workshops on creative and personal growth practices, eat delicious food, laugh and cry way more than usual and get a whole different look around their eyes. According to Becky, environmentalists spend an enchanted week at Hollyhock, fall in love with Cortes Island, buy land and drive up prices beyond the reach of locals. Then they try to shut down the logging that has sustained the settler families for decades. For example, Lisa and her husband couldn't afford a place of their own. They lived with their two kids in a small house on her parents' land.

There was a grain of truth in the theory. Years earlier a friend had shanghaied me to Hollyhock. I made a clay mask full of worry lines, then changed it to a smooth face with open eyes, ears and a big smiling mouth. I stayed up all night watching it harden in a fire on the beach. In the morning, an eagle dropped a small green branch in the ocean right in front of me, like a gift. I swam out to get it while the eagle watched from a tree. I played Hacky Sack in the parking lot with a gardener who threw it at me, hard, every time I apologized for my clumsiness. He told me about Linnaea's organic farming program, how he had learned soil science and planting by the moon cycles. Two years later, I returned to take the course where I worked hot and hard with friends in the production garden and then swam in the most beautiful lake I had ever seen. My husband and I bought 20 acres of land. I served on the triple crown of tree hugger community boards: the Linnaea Farm Society, the Hollyhock Lifelong Learning Centre and the Cortes Ecoforestry Society.

So I wasn't surprised when Lisa told me her mother didn't like me, but it still made me feel bad. Sometimes I wished that I had chosen public service that was less controversial, like the Volunteer Fire Department. Everyone knew that being a volunteer firefighter took discipline, knowledge and courage. Every Tuesday night, the firefighters drove the big trucks around the island and practiced disaster scenarios. But the Cortes Island Volunteer Fire Department had a redneck reputation. One of the firefighters even had a website devoted to accusations that Hollyhock was engaged in "eco-fraud."

Lisa's husband had just become the new fire chief. Like Lisa, he had friends among all the island groups, and people hoped that he could build bridges between the rednecks and the tree huggers. It didn't take long.

One February day in the school office, Lisa leaned across the counter and whispered,

"Did you hear?" Her voice rose on the "hear."

"The Firefighters' Easter Brunch is going to be at Hollyhock!" She gave her layered brown hair a proud toss. "The board just agreed."

"Wow, Lisa, how did you manage that?" I asked.

She gave a mysterious shrug.

"The firefighters' wives are going to love the tulip beds in the Hollyhock garden," she said, "and the rainbow chard."

I wanted to honor the way she worked toward her two worlds getting along. It took me exactly one second to think of how: a surprise visit from an anonymous Easter Hare.

It might not occur to everyone that this was the perfect thing to do, but the Easter Hare holds a special place for me. I'm impressed by the incongruous way it hops into a Christian holiday to hide chocolate eggs in gardens. Easter isn't a Christian name—it's a form of Eostre, a Mediterranean goddess worshipped since the Bronze Age. Even Easter's date is more linked to earthly seasons than Christian history: the first Sunday after the first full moon after the equinox. The Easter Bunny originated in Europe as the Moon Hare who laid golden eggs for children.

"Do you believe in Santa Claus?" my son asked me when he was four.

"I believe in him as the spirit of giving."

"I believe in him as a real person."

"Different people believe in different things," I said. "I believe in the Easter Hare."

"I guess Santa Claus is tops for me," he said, "and the Easter Hare is tops for you."

It was a good synopsis. If I hadn't graduated from receiving Santa gifts to giving them, I'd probably be as loyal as my son. But over time, Santa had become less of a nice guy who made the dark winter season more festive and more like someone debauched by the forces of commerce.

The Easter Hare's gifts kept giving, even to adults. The Hare personifies what actually happens in the spring. The hens start laying eggs again, and all those predictable miracles of seeds, leaves and baby birds start to unfold. I can induce a giddy joy in myself just thinking about it. I had always wanted to be the Easter Hare for children. This escapade would surprise Lisa and make her laugh.

I searched the Web for Easter Hare outfits, but all I found were white plush suits with floppy ears and silly grins. So I conspired with a local artist who immediately grasped the idea of the wild hare of springtime fertility. She made a huge papier-mâché head of a slightly intimidating creature with stiff giant ears and a cream-colored fuzz suit. When I crouched with a pillow stuffed in the back, my shape was distinctly hare-like. To maintain this look, I would have to crouch and hop. No walking.

Meanwhile, the logging conflict had heated up. The Klahoose First Nation had a reserve on Cortes Island, which is part of its traditional territory. The Klahoose had obtained a licence to log a woodlot on the island. Its management plan relied on the gold-standard form of slow, sustainable logging known as ecosystem-based forestry. A few trees were marked with blue paint, and operations were set to begin. The woodlot would be the first logging in a very long time that had broad community support.

But the very next week, a new Klahoose chief was elected who didn't agree with the sustainable logging plan. He decided to fast-log the Klahoose woodlot. The few trees marked for cutting under the old plan were to be left. The unmarked trees, the vast majority of trees intended to remain standing under the previous plan, would be cut. The Klahoose chief hired Lisa's dad, James McKenzie, to do the logging.

The former chief and the other Klahoose who had developed the plan for ecosystem-based logging decided to blockade the woodlot. They moved a camper van into the access road and took up residence there. They asked the non-native environmentalists to not join the blockade but invited us to stand at the side of the road in support when James McKenzie came to do his job.

James McKenzie came by every morning with a small group of men and politely requested access to the woodlot. The Klahoose blockaders, all women, politely refused. Every morning, I offered around muffins I had baked, a secret symbol of my belief in common ground. James McKenzie always refused my muffins.

Some of us spent a lot of time at the blockade, warming our hands over the fire barrel next to the highways yard. We cooked there and commented on the infrequent cars that drove the long, lonely road from one end of the island to the other. The organic farmers all had squeaky brakes.

During the weeks of the blockade, Lisa and I went for walks down the dirt road lined with dusty alders near the school. She had dark circles under eyes and wore her hair in an untidy bun. A big shirt covered her nearly to her knees.

"My mom thinks the environmentalists are using the Klahoose First Nation," Lisa said. "They're going to have the Klahoose log in that ecosystem way, which means not cutting any trees. Then they're going to take it over, log it all and get the profit."

"The woodlot belongs to the Klahoose," I said. "It's their woodlot, and using ecosystem-based forestry is their idea. Environmentalists don't want to clear-cut it. They want all the island forests logged slowly enough for the woodworkers to make things from the wood instead of the trees getting exported as raw logs. That would mean way more island jobs than just logging it all and sending it off the island."

I wasn't unsympathetic to the loggers. When I clerked for a federal judge during the spotted owl cases in Seattle, loggers snarled up traffic for blocks in their trucks loaded with huge trees. Their posters read "Your Starbucks cup" and "Your morning paper." It was a fair point.

But maybe solutions could be worked out on a small scale. The theories required a lot of assumptions: that people would pay more for truly sustainable wood; that urban outlets would want to sell artisan products marketed under a "Cortes brand," and that someone who loves marketing would show up to make all this happen, even though marketers don't seem to move to tiny communities at the end of the road. Nonetheless, clear-cuts and the export of raw logs were tantamount to exporting jobs. It didn't seem sensible, especially with the growing number of tourists on the island who wanted to hike the forest trails.

Lisa didn't buy it.

"That's what the environmentalists *say*." She didn't look at me. "Trees grow back."

I could feel the difference of what we had at stake: an idealistic vision and a father who wanted to go to work tomorrow.

A couple of weeks into the blockade, the Klahoose chief sued everyone, the blockaders in the road and the tree huggers at the side of the road. At the direction of a Canadian attorney, I prepared 50 affidavits and arranged for a notary to come to the village café for a mass notarization. Fifty disgruntled tree huggers huddled outside the café, clutched their lattes against the chilly fog and waited for their turn to sign.

A week later, the judge dismissed the case against the tree huggers and denied the request for an injunction against the Klahoose blockaders. He ruled they had the right to block the road because the chief had changed logging plans without the customary consultation. The Klahoose blockaders won—the chief would have to fully consult with them and the rest of their community. However, the blockaders owed thousands of dollars to their lawyer. To raise funds, they decided to hold a dinner and auction, the Saturday night before Easter.

The subject of the Klahoose fundraiser never came up on my walks with Lisa. That is to say, I never brought it up. You might say I avoided it. What was the point, I asked myself. Lisa wouldn't want to go anyway. It would just make her feel bad to know that all her friends were going. I wasn't hiding it from her. Maybe she already knew. I considered bringing it up at different moments, but none of those moments were the right moment.

The Klahoose blockaders rented the community hall and gathered auction items: carvings, paintings, boat trips and a trade bead necklace. They cooked sockeye salmon butterflied on stakes over open fires. Beautiful objects sold for extravagant prices, enough to cover legal bills and some of the protesters' lost wages. For one night, all barriers were down.

The next morning, my husband, son and I drove to Hollyhock for the Firefighters' Easter brunch. The scent of bacon wafted from Hollyhock's vegetarian kitchen. Gardeners of redneck and tree-hugging persuasions walked slowly down the bright sawdust paths and admired beds of giant tulips, magnificent heads of lettuce and the red, pink and yellow stems of rainbow chard. Everyone filled their plates with pancakes, bacon and eggs. Firefighters and environmentalists sat near each other at the tables along the deck that looked across the sea to the south, Hernando Island with a sandy scar left by a peeling cliff and flat, beige Mitlenatch Island.

Toward the end of the meal, I sneaked out to the cabin where I'd hidden the hare costume. I lifted the huge papier-mâché mask onto my head. It reduced the outside world to pinholes of light. I had a big basket full of organic chocolate eggs and some stuffed bunnies that I had gleaned from Vancouver thrift stores. To free up my hands, I tied the basket across my chest with a pink silk scarf. Hopping on all fours, always a challenge, required all my strength beneath the heavy, stifling mask.

I slowly hopped down the long path to Hollyhock's main lodge. The chamber around my head amplified my panting.

By the time I reached the front of the lodge, all the kids had gathered at the edge of the lawn to watch my approach. I stopped hopping and focused on sucking enough air to stay conscious. Eventually, I lifted my heavy head and waved it back and forth to see what I could see. Worried-looking kids encircled me, about six feet away. I hopped forward and tried to pat a little foot with my furry paw. The foot withdrew. I lifted my head and saw the child run to his mother, in tears. I threw a stuffed bunny after him. The kids sprang to life, and I tossed stuffed bunnies and eggs all around me while they scrambled on the ground. This excitement lasted about three minutes. The kids gathered around me again and started to ask questions.

"Are you really the Easter Bunny?"

I gave a rabbity affirmative grunt.

"Where do you live?"

I waved at the forest.

I noticed my seven-year-old son's shoes and looked up. He was staring at the back of my neck. Was my hair showing? Did he recognize the pink scarf from his play bin? Would he inadvertently blow my cover? Another kid reached out and tugged at something on my head. When he pulled his hand away, he held fur.

It was time to head out. I gave the kids a cheery wave and hopped ponderously along the dirt path toward the parking lot. The children followed me. I turned and waved again, more dismissively, and gave a slightly threatening "goodbye" grunt. They ignored this hint. They surrounded me, picking at my fur. I noticed a garden gate, hopped through, shut it behind me and leaned against it. This bought me a few sharp breaths. But as soon as I stopped blocking the gate, the kids were through. They sensed I was on the run, and their pursuit took on a slightly savage feel. I turned and feinted a charge. They dropped back, but not for long. I hopped through the garden as fast as I could until I reached the Hollyhock office. A bathroom! I hopped in and locked the door. The kids knocked.

"Come on out, Easter Bunny!" they called.

"Whatareya, scared?"

I set my giant rabbit head to one side, laid down on the floor and panted. My heart flung itself around in my chest. Sweat dribbled down my face.

The kids pounded on the door. Where were the adults, anyway?

Finally, I heard my friend Andrea's voice. "What are you all doing in here?"

"The Easter Bunny's stuck in the bathroom!" a kid yelled.

"Maybe the Easter Bunny needs some alone time," she said. "Go find your parents."

Bless her, bless her, bless her.

I listened to the kids shuffle out.

"Are you alright?" Andrea asked through the door. She didn't know it was me. I made a yes-like noise. I heard her close the door behind her. I was alone in the office. I removed my fuzzy suit, wrapped everything up in the scarf and delivered the costume to the truck. Then I returned to the lodge where people lingered at tables and sipped coffee.

"You missed the Easter Hare," my son said. He looked worried. He knew this would upset me.

"You're kidding!" I said, feigning disappointment. "I love the Easter Hare."

"It was kind of scary," he said.

My friends came over to our table, and my son wandered off.

"Have you seen Lisa?" one asked.

"No. She's here though, right?" I answered. "She must be."

"She isn't. I've looked everywhere."

This sank in.

"Uh oh," we all said, more or less together. "Maybe she's mad about the fundraiser."

"Maybe the Easter Hare can help," I suggested.

It dawned on them that I was the Easter Hare, and we hatched a plan to take chocolate to Lisa, who was presumably at home boycotting us for some reason having to do with the fundraiser. The four of us piled in a car, stopped at the store for a chocolate bar, and drove to the opposite end of the island.

We parked on the road outside Lisa and her parents' drive-
way, and I struggled back into the rabbit suit. I was going into
Becky McKenzie's territory hopping beneath a heavy head that
I could barely see or breathe through. That made me nervous.

"You guys are going to follow in a minute, right?"

"We're right behind you," they said.

I walked up to Lisa's door and knocked. Her little boy answered.

"Uncle Ralph!" he yelled. He pulled me in and climbed on
my back.

Through my pinholes, I saw Lisa sitting on the sofa in her
pajamas with red eyes and a box of tissues.

"I don't think that's Uncle Ralph, honey," she said. "Leave
the Easter Bunny alone."

I hopped to the sofa and presented her with the chocolate
bar. She looked unnerved, but she took it.

"Who are you?" she asked in an unfriendly tone.

Just then my other friends came to the door. I took off my
rabbit head. We tried to hug Lisa. After a little bit of resistance,
she let us. But she was still mad.

"You have no idea what it was like to learn about the fundraiser from my mom," she said. "She doesn't think I should
trust you to begin with, and then you didn't even tell me about
it. Why not? Why would you not even tell me? What else are
you hiding from me?"

"I thought about it a dozen times, but it felt so awkward
that I didn't," I said. "But you're right. I could make excuses, but
it's basically inexcusable to not tell a friend about something
they might want to know just because it's awkward. Friends
tell each other things."

Then I started to cry, and my other friends gave Lisa their
reasons and reassurances until we were all crying. This made
Lisa feel better, and she passed around the tissue and got us

each a glass of water. The quiet spring morning settled down around us. We chatted for a bit like usual, and then I put my rabbit head back on to leave.

Becky McKenzie was standing in her front garden with a shovel. She frowned at us as we tried to slink past.

"Who is that in the suit?" she called.

"It's the Easter Bunny," said Andrea, who used to be one of her friends back in the days when everyone got along.

"You tell the Easter Bunny that he's not welcome here, and I never want to see his face again."

I couldn't see very well, but I thought that maybe she shook her shovel at me.

I lowered my giant head, put my furry paws on top of it and skulked down the drive.

So, Becky McKenzie had kicked the Easter Hare out of her yard.

For an instant, the whole island population appeared to me as those who celebrate the Easter Hare's wondrous fecundity and those who threaten it with a shovel.

As the Easter Hare herself, I felt pretty righteous.

Then I realized that I could barely breathe and my exercise in bridge building had gone sadly awry. Maybe the more appropriate metaphor was one about being blinded and suffocated by my own enthusiasms.

Yet in that very moment another enthusiasm took hold, like one of those exuberant seeds we all take for granted that, unasked, lifts its green head from the dirt.

My next foray into McKenzie territory would be based on facts that Becky McKenzie and I shared. It would be noncontroversial public service. It would put James McKenzie and me on the same team. They would get to know me and realize that I wanted good things, not selfish things, for the island.

I would join the Volunteer Fire Department.

CHAPTER FOUR

Hail Mary, Shining Sea

BEFORE I WAS A Cortes Island homesteader or a lawyer, I worked as a registered nurse. My first job was in the San Luis Valley, a stark, windswept plain between two stately mountain ranges in Colorado. The hospital had one Mormon doctor who ministered to the Valley's primarily Hispanic population. The building squatted on the highway, an adobe-colored rectangle with a small sign swinging in the wind out front that read "Doctors needed." A nurse had scrawled "Single" across the top. My first patient was a ninety-year-old Hispanic woman tucked away in one of the hospital's back rooms.

Apollonia sat erect by the window, dying of leukemia. She could have been made of glass, except for the slowly moving rosary in her hand, the "*Dios te salve, Maria*" on her lips and the intensity with which she looked toward the Sangre de Christo mountains beyond. Every night as I helped her get ready for bed, she held my hands and searched my eyes and then spoke urgently to me in Spanish for five, ten, twenty minutes. I didn't understand anything she said until her rough English summary: "You are a *good* girl." But I wasn't a "good" girl, not by the Presbyterian standards I grew up with. My mother overlaid the rule of virginity until marriage with her value of a good figure and the ability to ignore unpleasant facts. These facts included my chubbiness and hypersensitive reactions.

Nor did I live up to the standards of Apollonia's Roman Catholic community. I had already shocked my neighbors twice, once by skinny-dipping in a creek with Charlotte Lujan while a logging crew spied on us from the hills, and another time by leaving Maria Trujillo's wedding with a handsome young poet. We drank wine, and I listened to him read Pablo Neruda in the Spanish I longed to understand.

"You can feel the meaning without understanding the words," he said, "as with music. English talks but Spanish sings."

But I even disappointed him by refusing to spend the night.

"What good is that?" he asked.

So when Apollonia held my warm, plump hands with her cool, bony ones, I didn't feel "good." I felt wonder at her incandescent goodness that made me, a young stranger, feel so loved and accepted. I wished I could understand everything she told me night after night. I swore to someday learn her language.

Two decades later, my own ideas of goodness had grown, mostly from moments when the natural world meshed with my inner landscape: a marsh wren's buzzy call that sang the calm, excited love growing between Barry and me as we nestled in the cattails; three dolphins the size of small cars who swam beside me offshore as if they liked my company; the bone-melting song of wolves that sounded like a chaotic version of "Amazing Grace." My idea of "goodness" had to do with belonging in a small yet reciprocal way to something huge and beautiful beyond my understanding.

One Cortes morning in 2005, I lay in a brass bed in a small yellow bedroom with a window that looked out at dripping cedar trees. My nine-year-old son read *Tintin in Tibet* beside me on the bed. I flipped through a pile of old *New Yorkers* and settled on a series of articles by Elizabeth Kolbert called "The Climate of Man." Kolbert had gone with climate scientists and anthropologists on their fieldwork trips and written about her conversations with them.

The first article described an Alaskan village that had to be moved from its ancient site on an island because global warming had melted the sea ice that had protected it from storm surges for centuries. The second article described cultures whose disappearances were linked to climate change, like the Akkadian Empire that was destroyed 4,000 years ago due to drought and crop failures. She interviewed scientists whose modelling shows much of the US suffering droughts in the future. The third article described how the Dutch government prepared for climate change with TV ads and buildings that could float, while George W. Bush ignored the problem. Kolbert concluded that available solutions wouldn't be implemented unless companies had to pay for their carbon dioxide emissions.

The series ended with this statement:

> It may seem impossible to imagine that a technologically advanced society could choose, in essence, to destroy itself, but that is what we're now in the process of doing.

Kolbert's matter-of-fact tone scared me. I've never responded well to people who try to convince me of things, perhaps because I spent so much time in church as an unwilling child. But understanding physical consequences that are well underway can terrify me, like the dentist who observed that of course my gums were receding because I clearly never flossed. Decades of dental admonishment didn't have the same force as that one neutral observation that catapulted me into regular flossing.

The greenhouse effect hadn't worried me any more than the other environmental problems. And Elizabeth Kolbert certainly didn't tell me that I should do anything about it. She just described her conversations with scientists who were increasingly alarmed. Reading those conversations alarmed me.

Maybe dramatic conversion is in my nature: from dental tragedy to fanatic flosser, from comfy mama to climate hawk. I realized that my effect on the world was different than I had imagined. We recycled, composted, rode bikes and grew food. But fossil fuels had never even entered our equation.

I looked at my son, his broad, smooth cheeks and how he moved his lips as he read. What did it mean for him, that the world had more carbon in the atmosphere than at any time in the history of humanity?

I tore out the articles and gave them to my husband.

We both understood that the information changed everything.

I love that about us.

We set a goal to quickly get our emissions down to the world average (a quarter of what the average American or Canadian emits) and then work from there to cut them in half over the coming years. Barry makes data management into an art form, so he created a spreadsheet and a colorful chart that estimated our yearly direct fossil fuel use and how much carbon we put into the air as a result. We sat at the kitchen table to discuss the results.

Our house meanders up a hillside, so we looked out over the orchard toward the forest beyond. Our son reigned in his Lego corner, a complicated city with restaurants, an airport, a fire station and a hospital, each with a huddle of Lego people working through a scenario. We used Barry's chart to plan the changes we would make over the next year: sell the Subaru wagon and buy a Prius, line dry our clothes, ride our bikes more and choose electricity over natural gas whenever possible. These simple measures made a huge difference. Our direct emissions per person (except for our flying) fell below one and a half tons per year.

Except for flying—that was our not-so-minor stumbling block. The single largest source of emissions in our spreadsheet was a trip to Europe, four tons each. Just flying to Los Angeles resulted in about one ton of climate pollution for each of us. Our vacation flights exceeded an entire year's worth of climate-safe emissions in just a few hours.

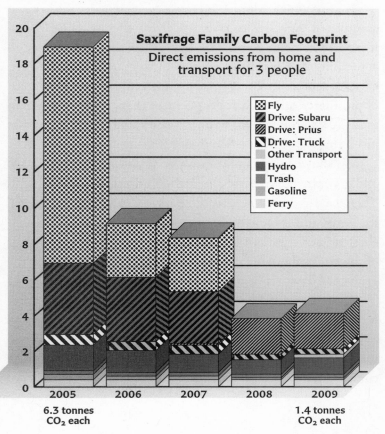

But of course, we *had* to fly. We had based our decision to live on a remote Canadian island on the assumption that we would fly to see our faraway family and friends. Not to mention our trips to Hawaii or Mexico to charge us up for a few more months of dim light and heavy rain. Every four years or so, we took a big trip to explore the world. Traveling recalibrated our appreciation for the good fortunes of North Americans. How could that be bad? Besides, everyone flew. Travel stories swapped with friends illustrated our adventurous spirits and interesting tastes. It just wasn't reasonable to give all that up. What difference would it make for us to not fly? As a practical matter, none.

But for some reason, it did make a difference to us. We had committed ourselves to trying to live a climate-safe life, and it seemed fickle to go back on that because we felt entitled to something that we admitted was a luxury. Aside from flying, existing renewable energy technology could power every part of our lifestyle. We didn't *need* climate change. We didn't want to say "Climate change is wrong." We wanted to say "We can be just as happy without those things that are causing it."

We showed our family and friends *An Inconvenient Truth* and gave them our chart and carbon offsets as a holiday gift. Then we decided to fly after all. Barry's mom had been unwell for years, and it looked like she might die. My mom was celebrating her eightieth birthday. The train would eat up half of my son's school break, and we weren't even considering the grime of Greyhound, not yet.

So we flew to California again. Barry was with his mother for the last few weeks of her life. I saw her long enough to tell her how grateful I was that she raised such a remarkable, kind man. My son got his first experience with death, that strange combination of grief and a hundred pragmatic decisions. All the photos and stories helped him know his grandmother as she was for most of her life before her illness, a vibrant woman who listened in a way that made others feel accepted.

One evening Barry and I walked along the beach. Nine pelicans glided just above the cresting waves. It reminded us of that expansiveness that we couldn't put words to even as we chose to let it shape our lives.

After that, we stopped flying. I had to reassure myself that my need for adventure could still be met, so I headed south on a Greyhound bus on a six-day trip to La Manzanilla, Mexico, a fishing village with a "natural language school." In memory of Apollonia, I would finally fulfil my promise to learn Spanish.

But what would Apollonia have made of the young men in the bus seat in front of me as we pulled out of Portland, Oregon, in a snow storm? An ornately embroidered baseball cap peeked over the seat, covered with silver and gold dollar signs, dice, cards and crowns.

"I love bacon," Las Vegas cap told his friend. "I wanna die eating bacon."

"I wanna die having an orgasm," his friend said.

"I wanna die eating bacon with a girl on top of me," Las Vegas cap chortled.

He repeated it a few times.

I felt ambivalent about my fellow travellers, the 40 people crammed into a bus with sticky floors. But they were closer to a sustainable carbon budget than my family and friends who conscientiously compost, recycle, commute by bike and, with their love of world travel, put a huge amount of carbon into the air. A study out of Princeton put a point on the problem: the world's wealthiest 8 percent, the 500 million people with an income of more than about $40,000, emit 50 percent of the carbon into the atmosphere.

My ambivalence about the bus cohort dissipated four days later when we crossed the Mexican border. According to my research, the kindly, middle-class Mexicans on my bus had near-sustainable carbon emissions. They filled their ample seats with dignity. The immaculate Mexican bus had only 30 seats, which meant I could stretch out my legs and turn the seat into an almost-bed. The TV screens worked and showed Hollywood movies. I'd already seen *Across the Universe* once, and it was showing again already.

Out my window, there were other buses, freight trucks, a burro and cart and very few cars. The flat landscape with dusty rock outcrops didn't change for the 12 hours it took to reach Chihuahua. A man traversed the spotless expanse of the bus station's stone floor with a mop, hour after hour. Bus company booths lined the walls, like airline desks at an airport. I chose one of Mexico's luxury bus lines, the Turis Star company that bragged, "Only twenty-three seats."

At the bus door, a young woman in a uniform handed me a water bottle and a sandwich: Wonder Bread and American cheese with a jalapeno plunked in the center. The bus filled up except for the seat next to me. In fact, no one had sat next to me since my arrival in Mexico. I spent my bus time knitting, listening to my MP3 player, guarding my stuff and putting certain thoughts out of my head, like drug wars, theft and being held for ransom. It took me awhile to notice that people were avoiding me and my stuff. They respected my gated community of one.

Or maybe the other passengers didn't want to sit near the incredibly hot heater vent next to me. I had nightmares that night of a little cartoon man from one of my Spanish books, stout and balding with sweat flying off him as he ran in circles yelling "Hace calor!" It's hot!

I needed off the bus so I found a hotel room in Guadalajara. In the artisan district, a skillful woman compelled me to exchange a wad of pesos for a beautiful shawl crocheted from crimson ribbons, my style in fantasy only. A five-piece Mariachi band in the hotel lobby played for me alone. When a horoscope scroll from a newsstand translated into something like "Your decision to leave quickly count with heavenly favors permit to unlock new course," I bought my bus ticket to La Manzanilla.

The bus from Guadalajara had 36 seats, a golden mean of comfort and carbon efficiency. The landscape finally shifted from burnt brown desert to green fields and pastures. We sped under brightly painted arches in pretty little towns. The driver alternated touching movies with music so sentimental that I wept. Rows of blue agave plants shot past like bursts of silvery blue stars. I was no longer merely trying to get somewhere. I had arrived at a state of contented journeying. I was on the bus.

In La Manzanilla, I dragged my duffle through the pebble courtyard of a pizza restaurant, dropped into a leather seat on the patio and ordered a Pacifico beer. The bay sparkled like Mary's sacred blue robes covered with sequins. In unison, 12 pelicans plunged into it with a force that should have broken their necks. But they bobbed up, gulping fish. Wooden wind chimes clunked a scattered tune. I closed my eyes as the achingly bright sun triggered an intense cascade of chemicals through my light-starved brain. Cool beer in hand, I leaned my head against the top of the chair, immobilized by pleasure.

Eventually, I hoisted myself out of the deep chair, trudged next door through the sand and found the American hostess of my bed and breakfast in a bathing suit, lying face down on a towel. She showed me my little room overlooking the main street to the back. Pictures of Frida Kahlo and her monkey challenged me from every wall. What was I doing here? Frida demanded. Was I creative and passionate? Did I love indigenous culture? What were my views on industrialization?

Like an acolyte, I decorated one of Kahlo's frames with my new crimson shawl. Then I went across the street for food supplies. I sat at the little table under Kahlo's stare and dug my spoon into what I thought was yogurt but was, in fact, sour cream.

The Spanish classroom perched high on a hill, open on the side that faced the turquoise bay. Victor, the skinny, seventy-year-old founder of the school, vibrated with intensity when he talked about the natural method of learning Spanish.

"We each have two kinds of memory," he said. "One is for rote memorization and the other one for pattern recognition."

He demonstrated pattern recognition by jabbing at the whiteboard with the tip of a felt pen, about 60 dots in the space of 20 seconds.

"What do you see?" he demanded.

I squinted at the dots.

"A swarm of insects?"

He looked surprised and stepped back to see the dots himself. Then he jabbed at the board about 60 more times, even faster.

"Now?" he urgently inquired.

"Dots," I admitted, "just dots."

"A face!" he exclaimed.

Sure enough, eyes and a nose popped out of the dots. He shook his head.

"You are the only person I've ever drawn this for who hasn't been able to recognize the pattern," he said.

He explained the importance of pattern recognition memory, how it allowed our ancestors to retain the massive amounts of information necessary for gathering edible plants in the deep past.

"The part of the brain used for rote memorization," he said, "is a puny evolutionary afterthought. Your success with Spanish will rely on pattern recognition. Do not use rote memorization. It will paralyze pattern recognition." He waved his bony finger at me.

Forgoing rote memorization seemed like a good idea, given my proximity to a beach. Unburdened by my book of 600 verb conjugations, I strolled along the sand toward the far end of the bay. Once past the handful of fishing boats and seaside restaurants, I stripped to my swim suit and immersed my pasty January body in bright warm water. I rested on the sandy bottom and looked up at the diamonds of light that wavered above me. I dove for a smooth round stone on the ocean floor, dropped it from the surface to watch it undulate down into a puff of sand and retrieved it again, several times. Offshore, humpback whales sang their songs with deep musical squeals.

Further down the beach, a deserted *palapa*, four posts in the sand with a thatched roof, offered shade. I laid out my towel and began my deep brain work. Dozing, you might say. But with the intention to find a way to live with the wound of climate change. What meaning did my life have when, in Elizabeth Kolbert's words, my society was choosing to destroy itself? It felt unbearable. Yet the ocean lulled me, and the warm sand held me up.

After a week of morning classes and palapa afternoons, Frida Kahlo kicked me out of my apartment.

"Just because I'm being romanticized by your gringa land-lady," she glared, "does not mean that you are having a Mexican experience. This is not Apollonia's part of town."

She was right. The road into town was paved and lined by vacation rentals and large restaurants with menus in both English and Spanish. It felt so familiar, the English speakers chatting with each other about the other places they had been or wanted to go. I spent time with a woman I knew from a yoga class in Vancouver. The Spanish school was in the front part of town as well, and my classmates were two nuns from Chicago.

The paved road led to a plaza lined with small restaurants, shops and food carts. It was a shared zone, where tourists rubbed elbows with locals. Once a week, everyone converged at an outdoor market with vendors from other towns who set up stalls to sell pirated DVDs, useful plastic items from China and traditional pottery.

Past the plaza, the paving stopped. I looked down the street and watched women sprinkle the dust down with a hose and sweep their high narrow sidewalks. Children ran down the street to school in white shirts and blue pants. Men talked in groups of two or three, and older kids toted plastic bags of groceries from an unknown store. The neighborhood had a sense of purpose that my part of town lacked. I didn't want to walk that street just to gawk and be gawked at. I wanted to live there. So I asked Victor for a homestay with a Mexican family, somewhere on the far side of the plaza.

The window of my cinder block room looked into a large mosaic grotto where my host Andreas placed more tiles every day after work: sting rays, starfish, dolphins and dozens of others creatures set in a sea of blue glass. In the corner closest to the street, tiled steps led up to an altar. A mosaic Mary presided over the sea creatures in aqua robes that shone like the sea.

In the evenings, the mosaic grotto became the neighborhood restaurant. My hostess Chayo flipped *hamburguesas* from a cart in the dirt street out front. Neighbors packed into plastic chairs to watch the *telenovella*, or soap opera, on the TV that hung in the corner of the grotto. I sat among them with a cabbage-filled quesadilla spiced with Chayo's addictive salsa, peanut butter blended with hot sauce. I watched the villain force the heroine with waist-length curls to dig her own grave, night after night. Chayo's four-year-old daughter crawled over me with dirty feet and charmed me with *secretes* that I could not understand.

By Canadian standards, we lived on top of each other, with very little square footage to call our own. But there was spaciousness in how I could move from the dining room full of people to my little room and back again without making a ripple.

But maybe that was because I couldn't talk to people. I couldn't even negotiate the meals that were part of my homestay. One Sunday evening, Chayo's cart never opened, and so I had no dinner. I changed into my sleeping clothes, a pair of soft, holey shorts and a soft, threadbare tee shirt. I brushed my teeth at the restaurant sink just as Chayo stormed in, dressed in a tight sparkly shirt and pants. She asked if I was hungry, and I said yes, hoping the cart would appear and I could eat my usual quesadilla. Instead, she marched me down the dirt street to one of the little restaurants on the town square, placed some food in front of me and waved goodbye. I sat alone in my tattered and transparent clothes while Mexican families strolled the square in their sparkling church finery. When I tried to scoop up a mysterious squishy substance that Chayo had bought me for dessert, I felt unaccountably happy.

Every day, I walked to the English-speaking side of town and up the hill to Spanish class where tiny words like *se*, *te* and *le* swarmed like insects with no discernible pattern. The two nuns from Chicago knew all about these little words. I suspected them of disobedience, of memorizing grammar on the sly.

Not me. I virtuously rode my rental bike down the beach to the deserted palapa for my regimen of intentional dozing. I probed for my ancient brain that would suck up language patterns like the leaf patterns of edible plants. I held my breath underwater and felt ocean vibrancy press into my pores. I read my Spanish lessons and waited for the patterns to emerge.

But the patterns didn't emerge, and I had only one week left at the school. I had to break the rules. The next time I headed to the ocean, I slipped my book of verb conjugations into my backpack. Lying in the shade of the palapa, I devoured page after page of verbs. I savored them. I repeated them. I memorized.

The very next day in class, I recognized the structure of the lessons. All those dialogues were examples of past, present and future tenses. Most of the little words were attached to reflexive verbs.

The day after, I haltingly conjugated verbs. The nuns watched in awe as I pieced together simple past, continuing past and future tenses, like I was a ten-year-old taking her first steps.

I explained to Victor in Spanish that I took the bus to Mexico because airplanes emit too much carbon.

"*Esta es una buena razon,*" he said. "This is a good reason."

That afternoon, I talked to my host Andreas in Spanish about his mosaic grotto. He told me how he moved to the United States for higher wages, but the cost of living was too high to save any money so he came back home.

"I don't save money here either," he said in Spanish, "but at least I can fish from the beach after work or create my mosaic."

In the evening, familiar words popped out of the soap opera dialogue. Neurons clicked into place, forming bridges between direct and indirect prepositions. My brain felt hot with connectivity.

The morning before I left, I drew a picture of the mosaic altar to the Virgin Mary in my journal and asked my hostess Chayo to sign it.

"*Sera mas significativo para mi,*" I told her, "It will be more meaningful for me."

She stared as if seeing me for the first time. Then she charged out of the grotto and came back with a gift, a big seashell with a plastic Virgin glued to it.

"You will come next year?" she asked.

I counted the years until my son graduated from high school.

"I will come in six years," I said.

"Six years!" she exclaimed.

"It's very far from Canada," I said. "Too far to travel very often."

She nodded as if she knew just what I meant. Her flying guests might come every year, but for the two of us, Canada was not an easy place to reach. Then she offered to arrange a ride to the town with the bus station.

Twenty minutes later, a red pickup full of boisterous young men pulled up in front of the grotto. So this is how I get kidnapped, I thought. Chayo caught my expression and looked so worried that I had to laugh. The ideas of dangerous brown men and racist white women collapsed into a heap of road dust as the boys in the truck bed eagerly made room for my duffle bag.

The driver couldn't wait to ask me what I thought of the newly inaugurated President Obama.

"*Penso el es muy bueno por Los Estados Unidos,*" I said, I think he is good for the US.

"*Y por el mundo,*" the young man answered. "And for the world. Because he is Moreno, brown like us, we feel trusted. The world feels different now."

We crested the hill that pressed the fishing village into a line along the bay. The sea shone a myriad of blues below us, like Andreas' mosaic grotto. I loved how his Mary reached out to the sea creatures, as if the natural world was an extension of herself. Maybe she was the Mary that Apollonia had praised as she gazed toward the mountains and prepared for death. Maybe Apollonia hadn't misunderstood who I was when she told me I was "good." Maybe, to her, I was part of a shining sea.

CHAPTER FIVE

Deep Blueberry Gestalt

A PARADE OF horribles marched beside me as I walked through the forest: desperate bears, violent men, twisted ankles. The imagined dangers struck primal nerves so I reminded myself that I was safer hiking alone in Strathcona Park on Vancouver Island, BC, than driving a car on a freeway. The protective measures at hand were largely ceremonial: a whistle tied to my pack and a Swiss Army knife in my right front pocket. The parade rattled alongside me until it got muffled by the peaceful emanation of the trees and wandered away. My legs sprang forward up the trail, lungs soaking in oxygen rich with green flavors: Douglas fir tree, huckleberry bush and foam flower.

It took four hours to reach my first campsite, two small muddy lakes. I raised the tent on a rocky outcrop and hung the food from a tree, beyond the reach of bears. The distant nuthatch's "heh, heh" sounded like my friend Lois chuckling. I swam and hunkered flat on the warm rocks to evade the cool breeze. Tiny bugs wavered in an invisible box, and downy white seeds scudded past. I found my pad and pen and wrote lists: a worry list, a gratitude list, a list of what I wanted to do in the fall. I noticed that my husband was on all the lists. So was my twelve-year-old son.

He appeared in my mind's eye, more clear than he ever appeared at home. My love had a flavor of anger. What was that about? At twelve, he didn't want physical love from me anymore. He dodged and pulled away. During his early childhood, love dwelt throughout our bodies. Now, it seemed submerged by arguments over computer time, sunscreen and chores. I didn't know what to make of him, his frustration, his grace. A wholly different creature had taken root in him, someone I didn't know yet, a new person without an acolyte's love.

That night, I lay with my knife and headlamp at hand and listened for scary sounds.

Silence.

I opened my book of interviews with Arne Naess, the Norwegian philosopher who built a stone house by hand in the mountains. In my twenties, his most famous term, "deep ecology," gave me a worldview that holds nature, rather than humans, at the center. As stars appeared through the netting of the tent, I found companionship in Naess's words.

The next morning, I hung up the dew-soaked tent to dry and basked in sunlight frosted by breeze. My metal cup held a tablespoon of instant coffee and six tablespoons of hot chocolate.

I read Arne Naess's idea of "possibilism," that we must decisively come up with our view of life and find meaning in it, yet remember that more things are possible than we can imagine.

It offered a way to just decide on a guidebook already, amidst my ongoing attempt to give my life a coherent narrative. And a way to accept that, even after 50 years, it was okay if my answers were still just guesses

In Arne Naess's example, angels could appear and change his view of everything. Although I am on terms with an undefined kind of angel myself, it annoyed me that Arne Naess illustrated his point with popular ephemera. It reminded me of a friend who, when I described climate change to her, suggested that friendly aliens might rescue us if the Earth became uninhabitable. "We don't *know* what will happen," she said.

Of course, Arne Naess advocated reliance on one's own hard-won view of life and not on angels that may not appear. The title of the book *Is It Painful to Think?* suggested his own vexation with a culture in reverie. But the angel thing bugged me. The world has physical truths that need to be faced head-on. I got up, gave the tent a vigorous drying shake and added more water to my chocolate slurry. A few mosquitoes rose, too cold and drowsy to bother with me.

I returned to Arne Naess, his distinction between life's complexity, built on meaningful relationships, and life's complication, built on confusing ones.

I had to admit, my life felt complicated. Unhappiness riddled our beloved little alternative school. Barry and I both worked there, true believers in the school's mission. But on a practical level, the small budget and low salaries discouraged the staff. As business administrator, I felt responsible. And enrolment would go down the next year. My three best friends had just withdrawn their kids. They broke the news at a women's getaway weekend, and I spent quite a bit of time sobbing on the couch. They had to do what made most sense for their families, but I could see a whole line of dominos that would fall, the tighter budget, the strain on teachers, the possibility that the school would close. In any event, our family needed to move the next year when our son reached high school. Where would we go?

I shook my head back into the bright alpine morning and the questions of the moment: Is the tent dry? Am I ready to walk? Wonderful simplicity! I rolled up the tent, packed the pack, put on the boots and walked.

Within ten minutes, I reached two big sparkling lakes, the ones I had been aiming for last night. I had made my best guess, failed to imagine bigger lakes, and so I camped at unnamed tarns: possibilism in action.

As I strode past the lakes, my thoughts returned to my son. I wanted to keep him safe, maybe a decorated cage, with ample monitored free time, healthy food and plenty of fresh air, a cage so nice that he'd never notice the Internet pornography, cigarettes and marijuana that lurk in the shadows of the free world.

I knew what I was supposed to do: support him and trust him. Yet, how to transform my repetitive worries with such vague principles? I needed true alchemy: better possibilities to bubble up from my subconscious and nudge open my mind.

A pebbly creek prattled below me. Pale green beards of moss drooped from high branches. The blueberry leaves appeared either purple or green, depending which layer of color I focused on.

After slipping past Panther Lake, unmolested by the cougars that bristled behind the bushes, I walked out of the forest onto a high plateau of ripe, wild blueberries. I laid down my pack and rustled through the bushes on my hands and knees, feasting like a bear. The ripest berries tasted like bananas. My knees were wet. Tarns flowed slowly past. An insect hum vibrated the lapis sky. I was five. I was fifty. I was balanced in the middle of the world.

That night, I returned to the human realm, camping on one of 30 wooden platforms at Circlet Lake. Big metal lockers protected bears from food. Green plastic ribbons marked heather re-vegetation areas. With six platforms occupied, it felt like a city. I kept my head down and headed out quickly in the morning to climb Mt. Albert Edward. My pocket held a stone to leave at the top, a ritual of my intention to become the mother my son needed. I couldn't picture her, but she had remarkable calm and certitude.

After an hour and a half of braided, muddy ruts, I reached the saddle between Mt. Albert Edward and Jutland Mountain. On a snow patch, ten young women stepped gingerly across the snow. The guide called them to one side so I could pass.

"What kind of group is this?" I asked him, looking at the stretchy pants, tight pastel shirts and clean swinging hair.

"Outward Bound. It's a girls' school from Toronto on a ten-day trip," he answered. "Where are you from?"

"Seven days with my family on Phillips Ridge, then three days alone starting at Forbidden Plateau. I'm heading out at Paradise Meadows."

"Nice," he said.

We discussed the route for a bit while the young women looked me up and down as if my shapeless clothes and leather boots made me a new third gender.

From the top of Mt. Albert Edward, I could see Campbell River and Comox to the east and the big peaks of Strathcona Park to the west. Clear-cuts to the north and south created that weird British Columbian juxtaposition of absolute splendour framed by devastation.

The wide-open peace reminded me that people have always come to mountaintops to pray. On a plain summit surrounded by snow peaks, I could imagine angels.

I now had three stones in my pocket, one for each member of my family.

May my family be safe, protected and happy.

I nestled the stones together in a hollow.

Heading down, I passed one of the boarding school girls half-way up the escarpment. She panted and held her long brown hair off her neck, her white shirt stained with sweat.

"Is the top worth it?" she asked.

"Totally worth it," I said. "You can see everything."

We smiled at that. I looked at the rest of her group milling about at the base of the slope far below and felt proud of her.

It was still early enough to climb Mt. Frink, which adjoins Mt. Albert Edward to the southwest. I left the trail to avoid the growing number of day climbers and headed down a field of crumbled brown rocks dotted with thick black lichen.

The sole of my leather boot started flopping at the toe. I had super-glued it once already in town. I stopped on a stone outcrop to reglue it, aware of the toxicity held in my tiny tube. "Sorry, sorry," I muttered, careful not to drip.

As I continued down, seven rackety ravens flew from the distant peak of Mt. Frink straight toward me. A few feet in front of me, they sharply veered to the southeast. It seemed completely purposeful, like a message.

"Okay, okay," I thought, heading a bit south, "I'll humor you."

The ravens landed on a rocky outcrop on the skyline to the southeast and watched me. Then one took off, flew at me and again suddenly veered away to the southeast.

"Okay, okay," I muttered, "I'll go to your rock."

When I reached their outcrop, they had flown, but I found a trail marker of piled rocks. I looked back to where I had fixed my boot: a boulder perched by the cliff edge. A tardy jolt of adrenaline made my legs feel weak. The rocky terrain had obscured my view of the empty air only a few feet away.

On reflection, I couldn't have walked off the cliff without noticing. Nonetheless, the ravens challenged my opinions about magical thinking. My friend who is willing to rely on aliens to save humans from death by climate change also thinks that, if you hold a certain state of being, the universe will provide what you want. But does that mean that people in Darfur or the Maldives have inferior states of mind? I didn't buy it.

But ravens had just intervened for my safety. Were they angels of a sort, agents of an obliging universe? Or were they just smart birds on friendly terms with hikers and desirous of their interesting food?

Ravens are corvids, an extremely intelligent family of birds. Groups of ravens are generally adolescents hanging out together to help each other find food. A gang of young ravens would know where humans usually walk and notice a human off the trail. It was kind of them to herd me back to the track. I left a few nuts on their rock to thank them, in case my guesses were right.

Unlike Albert Edward's trudge through rotting rock, Frink was a scramble up domes of glacier-scrubbed slabs and patches of snow. Water trickled through ten thousand tiny cracks. Two shorebirds with ruddy bright wings pecked at insects stranded on a patch of snow.

I had brought another stone to place on Mt. Frink's summit cairn. As I approached the cairn, it made a loud chittering sound.

An ant war! All over the stones of the three-foot cairn, winged ants battled. Black ants climbed onto the backs of red ants, pinning them with their wings while the red ants tried to bat them off. Reds outnumbered blacks, but the blacks were more aggressive. Amid tiny wins and losses, the balance of power remained stable. I set down my stone with a shudder.

A camper from the Circlet Lake campsite arrived at the top as I headed down. Like me, he wore a floppy-brimmed hat and tinted glasses. I considered people with these items to be part of an intellectual yet practical clan. He was probably a scientist.

"Ant war on the cairn," I said as he walked by. He gave me a puzzled look.

"Very nice too," he said in halting English.

I smiled, too embarrassed to explain, and headed down.

Back at camp, I sank my hot feet into Circlet Lake and delighted in the fact that no one expected me to cook a meal. I ate a couple of trail bars instead and went to bed. That night, I woke up hungry. If I got food from the metal bear locker, I would wake the other campers. Instead, I stretched out and watched the night sky. It was a good time for thinking. I started to tug on some of the weeds in my mind.

Growing old was one of my worries. But perhaps, if I had lost some opportunities to the passing years, age had honed my sense of purpose. I wanted to write in service of nature. I had waited a long time to be ready, and it was finally at the top of my list.

Regarding my son, I saw how my fears overlooked his complexity as a person. Did I trust him? I imagined his face, his eyes, and knew that my core trusted his core. And I could trust nature, the wisdom of evolution in him that would set him on his own search. Maybe I could get better at sifting real fears from general fears, his choices from mine. If I remained alert, I might be present when his love surfaced again, like an underground river.

I regretted the difficulties at my son's school, but liked being useful. People looked to me to be smart, honest and all in. I could sustain it for another year or two. It would take that long to plan for the coming transitions, for both the school and my family.

Under the unbound sky, all of this unfolded in the best possible way.

The next morning, I lay in bed reading while the other campers clanked and tromped their way out of camp. I had all day to hike nine kilometers. I could read in the sun at every lake on the way out.

Tiny waves sparkled across Mariwood, the first lake. I found a warm rock, pillowed my head on my pack and opened the book. Naess described the personal self and a larger Self. The larger Self comprehends the unity of the natural world and our part in that unity. From the larger Self, we feel the weight of human transformation on the natural world and desire our own lightness.

In that very moment, I tried to comprehend my unity with the natural world. It felt like a hum running through the greenery, the rocks, the trees, a brilliant place of no words. I hovered there, woven in with the lake and the sun. It felt exciting but hard to sustain. I slipped the book away and walked on.

A ways down the trail, a stooped and agile elder heading the opposite direction nodded at me with twinkling impartiality. I thought of an Alice Munro story where she describes certain old people as "clear-sighted but content, on islands of their own making." Like aging is as much about shoring up as letting go.

The surface of Croteau Lake shifted between gold, green and deep blue. The edges smelled rich with decay. I returned to Arne Naess and his description of the gestalt of experience, the layering of many different realities. The more layers one comprehends, he suggests, the more complex reality becomes. In his view, complexity of experience is achieved through simplicity of means. The less that is needed, the closer one comes to satisfying the ultimate goals of life. A lot of needs create vulnerability. I appreciated the elegance of this, how sustainability and self-fulfilment became two sides of the same coin.

A trout thunked. Across the lake, Mt. Elma shed giant rectangles of rock. Some of the slabs seemed to float in a separate, brighter plane, like Cezanne's Mont Sainte Victoire or Arne Naess's layered gestalt.

Back on the trail again, I met a couple heading the opposite way. The woman wore a sporty matching sweatsuit, like the ones my mom wore on informal occasions. Her smile broadcast that she was a very nice person. The man wanted to know where I'd been. I described my three days and nights alone.

The woman turned to her partner and said, "Well, if she can do all that alone, I guess I can get through this." She indicated the empty, dangerous forest with a dismissive wave of her hand.

"I was scared the first day alone," I told her, "but when nothing bad happened, I was just glad to be somewhere this beautiful." I gestured toward my treasure-laden wilderness.

She considered this.

"Do you know where I can find blueberries?" she asked suddenly. "I want to pick enough to bake a tart." She held out the Tupperware container in her hand.

I explained that if she turned left at Lake Mariwood, instead of right like most people, she'd find the high plateau of divine blueberries.

We exchanged blissful, understanding smiles.

Then she headed on her search for wild fruit, and I headed home, with clear intentions and a sense of possibility like the night sky.

CHAPTER SIX

Lagomorphic Resonance

I REACHED THE trailhead to Big Heart Lake at 2 PM on a bright, late September day to search for pikas, an adorable little relative of the rabbit that lives in alpine meadows. I knew that climate change had driven some pikas from their customary sites because they are sensitive to high summer temperatures and need a thick blanket of snow in the winter to insulate them from the cold. I wanted to make sure that my favorite pika colony still existed along a certain chain of lakes in the Cascade Mountains of Washington State where, in the past, I had spent hours watching them scamper around. How were they faring?

As I made the final adjustments to my pack, I realized that I had the rare opportunity for a John Muir hike. Muir, a famous American naturalist of the late 19th and early 20th centuries, traveled with only a wool blanket for warmth and hard tack for food. In storms, he danced through the night to stay warm. I'd always wanted to try it and, because I was hiking alone, I didn't need to convince anyone that it was a good idea. I could leave the tent and stove behind and hike lightly, quickly.

None of my food required cooking, except tea. Without morning tea, I would get a headache. I packed the stove. If it rained, I could bivouac under a big rock when I got tired of dancing. But was there such a big rock up there? I couldn't remember. So I packed the tent. It was a moment of truth: I might never fulfill the fantasies of a younger self, even though I could if I still wanted to.

Instead, I hoisted my heavy pack and trudged along the trail. Ten minutes later, I remembered my cell phone. My husband was sure there would be reception up there. I set down the pack, jogged back to the parking lot and grabbed the cell phone. No reception. But now the cell phone represented safety and connection. I stuffed it into an already full side pocket. So unlike John Muir.

My destination was a high shelf above the river valley with a string of lakes, each one more beautiful and less visited than the one before. I'd been there twice, once with Paul, a friend from high school who had died a few years out of university, and once with my husband and son. I kept imagining Paul. He was brown, slender and solid, like a tree trunk. He seemed to flicker on the trail like light moving through the trees, a presence and an absence.

The memory reminded me of a theory called "morphic resonance": that we are influenced by energy fields built through the repetition of thoughts and actions over time. It felt like some remnant of Paul and me, as we had been, remained in the place itself.

My thoughts turned to the objective of my trip: to see some pikas, those furry bright-eyed ovals with tiny round ears. They live in the high meadows where small plateaus fan out beneath slopes of broken-up rocks. Soil accumulates there, and water gathers into little brooks. In the summer, pikas mow the meadows with their teeth and dry their harvest in little piles on the rocks, hay for winter feeding. They perch on boulders to look around and call to each other with a high sustained "*eeeep!*"

Pikas' common names liken them to their cousins in the rabbit family, with whom they share the taxonomic order *Lagomorpha*: Boulder Bunnies, Rock Rabbits and Whistling Hares. Author Craig Childs describes pikas as "noble postured mice." Chipewyan Indians called them "Little Chief Hares," which captures both their dignity and their adorability. Even their Latin name incorporates nobility: *Ochotona princeps*, Pika Chief.

Maybe people honor them with such names because they are so small and yet endure such long mountain winters. Unlike the marmots who sleep three quarters of their life away up there, pikas stay active beneath rock and snow for the coldest months. They eat the hay they put by the summer before. Scientists figure that pikas make about 14,000 trips with their mouths stuffed with flowers and grasses. They choose a variety of plants, some with toxic constituents that act like preservatives when the piles get cached underground.

My husband Barry and I almost chose "Pika" for a last name, because it reflects our love of wild places and the happiness we feel when hiking around high meadows with field guides in hand. Instead we chose the name "Saxifrage," after the tiny white flowers that burst from stone crevices in those same meadows. We liked that the genus name *Saxifragaceae* means "stone breaker" in Latin, as if rooting and thriving in one's place can overcome the most obdurate substances.

To make the name change legal, we had to fill out a form and swear to an amused judge that we weren't trying to defraud our creditors. Our families didn't know what to make of our earnest explanations of how we were claiming relationship to those high, pure places where the pikas live.

As I hiked, I imagined a little wintertime pika in her dry cave under the rocks. Dim light might come through the snow mantle for a few hours each day, but more likely she carefully tends her hay pile in the dark. Maybe she sorts through her stack at each meal, pushing the toxic plants around for best effect. Maybe she crawls into the pile to doze. Her fingers and toes stay cozy warm because even their bottoms are covered with deep fur. Now and then, she defends her hay pile from a brigand pika. Maybe she pads through dark tunnels into her neighbor's yard on raids of her own. When she hears noise overhead, she goes perfectly still, hoping a weasel won't dig through the snow and eat her.

After about 4,500 hours under there, the glow from above increases and begins to last longer. She hears water dripping in a distant passage. She leaves her hay pile for a quick round of mating, or maybe several long ones. Then she gives birth to two, three, maybe four babies. She times it so that after she nurses them for three weeks there's enough new growth outside for them to get started on their own 14,000 hay trips. But not too close to her; they have to find their own territory. When she sees a hawk, or wants to greet her offspring, she gives a high, resounding "*eeeep!*"

Pikas seemed like one of the many improbable details of the world's enormous diversity. Species developed for such a long time and in such particular relationships to their places that, among countless marvels, bunny-like beasts make hay piles high in the mountains.

In 2007, pikas had a moment of fame, but it was for the worst reason: an environmental group petitioned the US government to list them as endangered due to climate change. One problem is hotter summers and warmer winters. Their thick fur makes them overheat in temperatures over 26 degrees Celsius, about 79 degrees Fahrenheit. Warmer winters mean more rain and pikas freeze to death in cold snaps if there's not enough snow to insulate their burrows. Another problem is that pikas live on "sky islands." To some extent, they can move higher to find colder habitat. But edible meadows are less common at higher altitudes and, ultimately, the mountains give way to air. Other mountains may offer conditions in which to thrive but pikas don't have the capacity to cross the valley from one sky island to another.

Then, in 2010, I read that the US government had decided to not list them under the *Endangered Species Act* after all. It found that the pikas that inhabit southern BC down to California live at both higher and lower elevations than expected, and there are plenty of them.

At first, I was relieved. Then I was suspicious. Listing pikas under the Act would give the US government direct responsibility for protecting their habitat. It had already declined authority to use the Act to tackle climate change when the Alaskan polar bear was listed as "threatened." But a pika officially endangered by climate change might seem closer to home. I suspected that the decision was part of the general reluctance to grapple with climate change and may not have been based strictly on biology.

I hadn't seen pikas in a while. Our recent family backpack trips were on Vancouver Island, which has never had pikas. I missed them, and I worried about them. I felt entangled with them.

A friend who rolls his eyes at "morphic resonance" gave me an article that described quantum entanglement: how experiments have shown that if two photons get messed together and then moved miles apart, whatever happens to one photon will instantaneously happen to the other photon.

"The entanglement theory is sure to be abused by new-age theorists," my friend sighed as he handed me the article. So I didn't pretend that "morphic resonance" or quantum entanglement gave a scientific explanation for the connections I felt while hiking that trail. But they certainly described my sense that what happens to the pikas affects who I am.

The trail climbed from the forest into a steep meadow. I felt strong in the end-of-summer way, fit but with occasional twinges through my knees, reminders of wear and tear from a season ardently spent out of doors.

A sudden, explosive rumble reverberated through the valley. Alarm chemicals flashed through my blood as noise tore the air. I sat down in the middle of the trail. After a few moments, two fighter jets streaked silently through the valley far below. The quiet filled in behind them. Oh, yeah, the fighter jets, I thought. I'd seen them every time I'd been here, as much a sign of this wilderness as the Indian paintbrush, valerian and arnica that brushed my legs along the trail. After the jets, everything seemed immobile, silent. Then I noticed the cool breeze turning the leaves of the vine maple, the sound of a river spilling off the cliff across the valley and the lowering sun. Dark splintered peaks above the meadow punctured the sky. I pushed myself up to my feet and lumbered up the rubble path.

When I reached Copper Lake, the first high lake on the shelf above the valley, I slipped my pack off, devoured a meal bar and poured water down my throat. At my feet, gobs of sap glistened on chunks of purple-green spruce cones. A squirrel seemed determined to upbraid me for as long as I rested, so I hiked on. The vanilla sweetness of tree bark suffused the air. From the high point between Copper Lake and Little Heart Lake, the jagged spires that had looked so imposing from below looked merely uncouth, unsmoothed by time.

I suddenly recognized where I stood. This was the very spot where, seven years ago, my husband and I had forbidden our eight-year-old son to say one more single world about computers. For hours, an incessant stream of computer fantasy blather had distracted us from where we were. This was our sacred annual trek away from the human house of mirrors into wild terrain. Could he just can it?

My son no longer shared his thoughts so freely, and I longed for them. We had fumbled such moments. I had regrets, but no grasp of the parent who I wished I'd been.

My hips ached and my feet burned. I had known this hike would be hard, an elevation gain of 1,400 meters in ten kilometers. I remembered all the things I had meant to bring but forgot: Scotch, aspirin and a spoon.

Around the bend, a work crew of two young men and a woman descended. The woman had dreadlocks. One young man looked grey and undernourished. The other, the apparent leader, looked like a small Tom Hanks. They carried six-foot hand saws in canvas covers, and pickaxes.

After formalities, I asked, "Are there pikas at Big Heart Lake?"

"They're everywhere here," Tom answered, "making their little hay piles."

"That's what I'm looking for!" I exclaimed. "Oh my god! I *love* the little hay piles!" I even clasped my hands and rolled my eyes.

Sure enough, a few hundred yards on, I heard several "*eeeep*"s. A slope of boulders tumbled down to a green meadow where a little brook took form, the perfect pika habitat that I had remembered. A pika called from underneath a pile of huge rocks right next to the trail where I stood. I waited for it to poke out its head. Instead, something high up the boulder field caught my eye, a sleek golden shape. It flowed down the rocks like a stick in a shallow rapid: fluid, honed fur, all the way down to where I stood. I groped for its word. Weasel? It darted in and out of the boulders in search of the pika. I could see vertical markings, like exclamation points above its eyes. Its tail and paws were the darkest gold.

"It's going to eat the pika," I thought with a gasp. The creature glanced at me, unperturbed. It flowed toward me and ebbed away, exploring my presence. I thrilled to the perfection of how its lithe body funneled into its sharp nose, its sharp nose into even sharper teeth. Those teeth—I clenched inside, and as if it sensed my tension, the weasel flicked away and disappeared into the rocks.

I found the word: pine marten! I had never even hoped to see a pine marten, thinking them shy and rare. It seemed an example of nature's reciprocity: if you come and make yourself quiet, you will learn secrets. It happens every time, somehow.

In ten more minutes, I reached Big Heart Lake. I pitched the tent on a little shelf across the lake from a pika field. It was our smallest tent: old, underused, stinking of rotting plastic. I kept the door unzipped until I woke up to: *skitter, skitter, skit-ter, plunk. Skitter, skitter, skitter, plunk.* An insane mouse was doing half pipes on the back of the tent, running until its little claws could no longer overcome the slope then falling back to the ground. I zipped the tent door halfway up, and the mouse appeared. It sat on the folded fabric and stared in. I batted at the door, and the mouse tumbled down. I zipped the tent all the way up into a smelly cave and listened to a few more half pipes up the front. The river sounded like a party with voices laughing and chattering over a scratchy phonograph. I could almost understand the words.

Night became complete. The pikas called to each other across the lake. Every time I awoke through the night, I heard them.

In the morning, the loudspeaker of solitude blared in my head. An inner voice clamorously narrated each step of the morning tea ritual. The overcast sky turned Big Heart Lake's movie star dazzle into dull grey. Mosquitoes clustered around me. A great blue heron tucked and dropped toward a lake far below.

I left camp for the boulder field. Little pika paths led toward round fairy-tale holes, but I heard no "*eeeep*"s. I settled on top of a giant flat rock above the miniature hay fields. After 20 minutes, a very bunny-ish pika appeared from the hole below, close enough for me to see tiny fluffs of white hair in its little round ears. We stared at each other, and then it scampered under a boulder. It reappeared about 12 feet further on. After another long look, it disappeared again, this time for good.

I wondered about its underground route. Was it a well-worn tunnel, or an unimproved jumble of rocks through which there were many passages?

I sat on my hot boulder and thought about the two different tracks of pika research. The US government relied on a study by Constance Millar and Robert Westfall in the decision to not list the pikas under the *Endangered Species Act*. Those researchers had searched far and wide for good pika habitat and then noted whether pikas actually lived there or not. The study was a one-time census of present pika populations and habitat, like a snapshot. It showed lots of them, living at higher and lower elevations than expected. The researchers concluded that pikas had plenty of cooler places to move to, if need be.

Other studies were based on repeat visits to known pika sites over a number of years and, in some cases, decades. Like a movie, it showed changes through time. Erik Beever, Chris Ray and others reached the opposite conclusion from Millar and her team: pikas were gone from some of their historical sites, particularly at lower, hotter elevations. The scientists saw their absence as a sign of declining populations although, for the moment, there are still a lot of pikas. Beever and Ray identified climate change as a new and potent driver of this decline and saw limited options for pikas to adapt. And the movie of the pikas' decline has just begun: even with immediate action, existing CO_2 in the atmosphere will mean an increase in summer heat and a decrease in winter snow for decades to come. The pikas are headed for hotter summers and rainier winters.

The pikas in my perfect pika field had squeaked their abundance through the night. But where the heck were they now? Did I not deserve chorus lines of boulder bunnies, me, a human who cares about them, a lot? I thought entanglement was a two-way street. But it didn't seem to work like that. Maybe pikas adapted to the heat by sleeping through the day. That would explain why I had heard them calling through the night. And it was darn hot for September. Little bugs were landing in my sweat.

I abandoned the boulder field and wandered along a high shelf. Across the water, a little peninsula jutted into the lake. Paul and I had camped there. For two days, we ate trout, blueberries and hot chocolate for breakfast and dinner. He made his green eyes go big as he tried to hold my hand for the 20th time. I pointed out, again, that he had a girlfriend.

"I'm just a kid in a candy store," he said, as if he had no choice in the matter.

He had died in the bottom of a crevasse on Mt. Olympus when he unroped from his climbing companions on a glacier so he could boot-ski down. I hoped he hadn't suffered. On Mt. Rainier, we had fought about that very thing: he wanted to unrope, and I refused to move until he tied in again. He believed in whatever got him what he wanted in the moment, and that blinded him to the danger. He took pride in saying that he would never grow up.

Well, you never did, I thought. I'd been mad at him for falling into a crevasse for 30 years.

Would this be a place to lay it to rest?

I tried to think of the good things about Paul. In high school, he drove a sports car and starred on the tennis team, yet he sought me out, a chunky nerd girl. On camping trips, he rolled his eyes in pleasure at every bite of trout, and every blueberry patch could have been the first he'd ever seen. I had hurt his feelings, but he still wanted to be my friend.

I miss you, Paul, I thought. I wish you were still across the lake from me, pulling in a trout for dinner. We got to do the good stuff together, the adventures, and we really appreciated them at the time. In my imagination, he flashed a bashful smile and cast his line again.

Back at camp, I rinsed off the muggy day in the lake and then sat in the tent out of reach of the mosquitoes. It was only four o'clock. Rain finally spattered down, and I was glad I didn't have to find a boulder to crawl under. I drowsed, woke up again at 6 PM, and took my camera to the boulder field. The pikas were all over the place, scampering across the boulders, giving their "*eeeeeep!*"s. I photographed a hoary old pika with a whitish ruff, and a perky young thing poised in the horizontal crack of a giant boulder. The pikas didn't dance for me, but they didn't avoid me either. We enjoyed the evening together, precious moments of perfect temperature.

The next morning, I packed and headed down the trail. The shabby trail crew was hard at work in the steep, rocky meadow. We exchanged stories about pine martens, pikas and climate change.

"The reason they know pikas get overheated and die is because they tried it in the lab," Tom Hanks told me.

"That's just wrong," I said.

"Yeah, I know. In another study, they took their hay piles. They survived, but I don't think they would in a winter where the snow stayed until July, like this year." He added, "Mostly we have less snowpack because there's more rain."

We looked at each other in silent acknowledgment of what this meant for pikas and embarrassment for our species.

As I descended, I wondered why some people would overheat a pika and others wouldn't. Why did I care so much? Maybe I had just turned them into a sort of meta-pet, something cute and fuzzy that makes me say "*aaawww,*" which I like to do. Maybe I just knew more about our common origins—the shared many times great-grandmother, who lived about 75 million years ago before lagomorphs and primates parted ways. Maybe I believed in a common fate, that a world too hot for pikas wouldn't accommodate humans very well either. If pikas went extinct, would my grandchildren sense an empty place in the morphic field? Each generation relies on a more denuded world to define changes to the Earth. But a few stories persist. I'd never seen rafts of ducks filling the wetlands or rivers brimming with salmon, yet I missed them.

By the time I reached the car, I felt more entangled with pikas than ever. I wanted to be a real saxifrage, hidden in a hay pile tucked into a stony recess under a thick blanket of snow, being pushed around by furry little paws.

CHAPTER SEVEN

The Oolichan and the Snake

Pipelines from the Alberta tar sands are a big deal in British Columbia, and I wanted to understand the opposition of the First Nations people. For one thing, the proposed Northern Gateway pipeline from Alberta to the port of Kitimat in northern BC would have to cross traditional territories to which they still hold aboriginal title because their ancestors never relinquished it. For another thing, the pipeline would offload bitumen into supertankers bound for Asia that would have to travel through some of the world's stormiest seas. An Exxon Valdez-type spill could destroy the livelihood of Coastal First Nations, the way it did for native Alaskans, only worse because heavy tarry bitumen would be even more impossible to clean up.

So I gathered a list of contacts from friends and friends of friends and got on a Greyhound bus that lumbered north for 20 hours into one of the coldest snaps in recent history. I leaned my head against the rattling window and ruminated on how 30 degrees Celsius below zero could kill me, with or without the shiny space blanket tucked in my backpack. The bus dropped me at the side of a highway in Smithers, and

I stepped gingerly along the huge dirty snowdrifts to cross the highway divider and check in at the hotel where a regulatory panel would listen to First Nation testimony on the pipeline the next day. Then I walked a couple of kilometers to the public pool to swim off the bus kinks. A thin sheet of ice sealed the community center door shut. My hair froze as I trudged home through a long parking lot adjacent to the main highway. A Tim Hortons shone bright, an oasis of warmth. I sat alone and munched my first doughnuts in decades. I never wanted to leave, and I understood Canada just a little bit better.

The next morning, about 60 members of the Wet'suwet'en First Nation entered the hotel's convention room. They beat round drums and wore regalia: black felt capes with red trim and elaborate animal designs of sequins or felt. Chiefs wore tall cedar headdresses lined with feathers and twigs. Everyone chanted, song after song after song. The three people on the regulatory panel watched from behind their table at the front of the room with polite, pained smiles. The Wet'suwet'en sung a song written for the occasion, first in their language and then in English:

> Our territory is our livelihood
> We live off our land
> Law, language, land
> Enbridge, don't step on our land.

The head of the panel, a pale blond woman with rectangular glasses, clasped her hands under her chin and reminded everyone that the panel couldn't accept opinions on whether they wanted the pipeline or not. The panel could only accept oral histories.

The Wet'suwet'en First Nation is good at oral history. It was one of the plaintiffs in the landmark Delgamuukw decision of 1997 in which the Supreme Court of Canada held that oral history is evidence of title, and aboriginal title is protected by the constitution. Every story the Wet'suwet'en told to the pipeline panel was crafted to a point, with just occasional outrage at the prospect of a pipeline full of bitumen crossing their unceded land.

When a chief rose to testify, ten to twenty members of the house and clan stood behind her or him, in clan regalia to show that their chief spoke for all of them.

"My grandfather taught me how to honor the day," one chief testified. "Then he showed me how to make a fish trap of spruce branches, how to make a trail to the river and how to set the net. It was a very spiritual process."

Another chief explained the feast system, banquets where food is redistributed, disputes are resolved, chiefs are chosen and debts are settled. "Whenever we hold a feast," she explained, "what happens at that feast becomes law."

A third chief recounted a strong earth quake that occurred when she was a child and asked what such an earth quake would do to a pipeline full of tarry bitumen that ran along a river with a salmon run on which they have relied for food since time immemorial.

Toward the back of the huge room, I sat with my laptop, a stranger taking notes. Each story pointed out fundamental differences between my culture and theirs. Hunting was subsistence, not recreation. Potlatches were government, not a social occasion with a random mix of food. Traditional territories tied it all together: access to food, family ties, governance, spiritual practice, heritage and legacy, an undivided whole. The Northern Gateway pipeline would run through their farms, parliaments, churches, graveyards, schools and across their dinner tables. It would plow through a culture that developed in pace with the rest of the living creatures of this place, with the salmon, the bears and the giant trees. When the glaciers first receded from the area 10,000 years ago, humans and other creatures flowed over the newly naked land to thicken it with vibrant life. The descendants of these people filled the room, and they were angry.

Nonetheless, the testimony had a tempered dignity. The Northern Gateway pipeline was one struggle in a string of many. Lined faces reflected hard lives. Most of the older people would have been forced into residential schools by the Canadian government. I'd heard some testimony of survivors at a reconciliation event in Vancouver: sexual abuse, living away from one's parents, bad food, tuberculosis, beatings, being treated like nothing. But these Wet'suwet'en had made their way back to their lineage and its ongoing responsibilities.

"Our land is who we are," one chief said.

The next day, I asked Lucy Gagnon, the manager of the Moricetown Band, to take me out to where her family hunts. She looked incredulous, then laughed.

"It's thirty-five degrees below zero out there," she said.

Instead, she parked her little car next to a giant waterfall and described how her people had netted salmon there for thousands of years.

"I can't fathom a world without salmon," she said.

She took me home and showed me her freezer full of salmon and a moose. She lifted a shrink-wrapped moose nose for me to look at, a special delicacy. Then she showed me pictures on her computer of her mother picking blueberries with her children.

"She likes to make up compliments as she picks," she said. "She tells them they have such beautiful eyes for blueberries."

The next day, I headed to Terrace, a city near Kitimat where the proposed pipeline would terminate. I asked the receptionist at a hotel if I could wait in the lobby for my ride. He said of course, as if everybody in the north lets strangers hang around inside so that they don't freeze to death.

Gerald Amos, an elder of the Haisla Nation, would pick me up. Friends in Vancouver told me I had to speak to Gerald—an eloquent writer and speaker and a really nice guy. His son had a basketball game in Terrace that night, so Gerald offered to drive me to the town of Kitimat on his way to Kitimat Village on the Haisla reserve.

Gerald seemed harried when he drove up in a little sedan. His wife Gail felt sick, so we searched for an open convenience store to buy ginger ale. Then we drove for an hour through the storm. The dark road and blowing snow weren't conducive to conversation, but I really wanted to ask Gerald about the oolichan, an oily little fish that was a traditional staple of Coastal First Nations. I'd read that, in the early spring, oolichan filled rivers to the brim and provided the first springtime feast, a much-needed replenishment after a winter of preserved food. First Nations made "grease" with some of the abundance, because it stored well.

To make this grease, they let the oolichan decay for a week to strengthen in flavor and release their oil. Then they add water and simmer the oil to the top. They ate grease on everything, from sweet to savory. It's rich in the right kinds of fatty acids and even good for the skin. Grandparents who ate it in traditional quantities often lived well past one hundred.

Deeply grooved "grease trails" still exist between the Coast and the Interior. For thousands of years, Coastal Nations walked these trails to deliver the precious grease to Interior Nations in exchange for delicacies like soapberries. A woman I'd met in Smithers said she still has a trading partner in Hartley Bay, grease for berries. A Haida man described how it felt to walk the trails made by 10,000 years of ancestors.

"The hair stood up on my arms the whole way," he said. "It was like they were still there."

According to legend, the first Haisla in Kitimat was a man banished by his village for accidently killing his wife. He found a place where no one else lived because it was close to a big monster that occasionally opened its mouth and made a deafening roar. After a while, the man felt brave enough to approach it. He found the "monster" was in fact a huge flock of seagulls swooping down to feed from a river tight with oolichan.

I'd wanted to try oolichan grease for two decades. There just had to be oolichan grease here among the Haisla. I finally got up the courage to ask Gerald for some. A long pause ensued.

"I told my wife that the official word is that we have no grease left," Gerald said.

We went quiet again.

They dropped me off at the only hotel in Kitimat. It had one room left. The innkeeper wore a lacy nylon shirt, lots of makeup and hair spray. I looked like a purple marshmallow in my down jacket. In the bathroom, the toilet paper wrapper boasted virgin fiber, no recycled content. It was thick and tightly wound, the luxuriant toilet paper of my childhood, not like the droopy eco-paper I now buy.

The next morning, snow still swirled from the sky. I asked the innkeeper if she would keep my bag while I went to the restaurant on the other side of the parking lot. I felt her eyes at my back as I struggled across the snowy humps until I safely opened the restaurant door. She reminded me of my friends in other rural industries, their pride in looking out for people's safety. I felt grateful. My husband has so much confidence in me that it would take a few days of no emails or texts before he got worried. If I fell into a snow bank, I'd be dead by then.

I struggled to open the huge timber-framed door into the restaurant. The restaurant itself seemed built at one-and-a-quarter scale, so the twenty or so tables looked small. Women managed their young children and men in reflective vests sipped black coffee and stared at the TV screen. I felt them not looking at me. Pictures of bears, canoes and sunsets hung on the log walls. The TV was muted, but the radio played a pop station with songs like "Rikki Don't Lose That Number" and "I Shot the Sheriff."

I found a booth away from the speakers and stared out the window. Gusts sent the snow in the parking lot spiraling into the snow coming down. An ad broke through the innocuous radio music:

> Stop foreign billionaires from sabotaging Canada's national interest! Foreign billionaires are hiring front groups to swamp the hearings to block the Northern Gateway pipeline project…. The pipeline promises thousands of jobs and billions of dollars for all Canadians. Whether we decide to go ahead with it or not, we get to make this important decision about our future— not outsiders. They don't answer to Canadians. They answer to their foreign paymasters.

Rousing music, then, "It's *our* pipeline. *Our* country. *Our* jobs. *Our* decision."

I looked around. Did anyone else find the ad disturbing? Could they tell I was an environmentalist writing about the pipeline for a progressive Vancouver news site?

The men just sipped their coffee, and the women kept trying to chat over their kids. No one looked up. Maybe they heard this stuff all the time. But had they heard any of the First Nations testimony on the pipeline? The Wet'suwet'en must find the talk of "foreign billionaires" insulting.

My mind drifted back to the restaurant carpet, the way it looked like green-and-cream salmon eggs from one perspective, and rows of splotches from another. I checked my watch. Just then, the door opened and Gerald Amos entered. I could see him more clearly than the night before, about sixty, with rectangular glasses. He wore a tan parka and a black cap with a red salmon on the front. He held the elbow of a tall, slightly stooped man in his eighties who wore a long black parka with a fur-lined hood. I knew this was Cecil Paul.

A friend from home had worked with Cecil on the Kitlope Heritage Conservancy. In the early 1990s, the West Fraser Timber Company planned to log part of the Haisla's traditional territory. Instead, thanks to efforts initiated by Cecil, the Kitlope Heritage Conservancy now protects the largest continuous tract of coastal temperate rainforest in the world.

"You must meet Cecil," my friend told me. "He's the loveliest man."

Cecil took my hand and peered at me through white-rimmed eyes. We spoke of our mutual friend, who is more energetic than six squirrels in a box. When we ordered food, Gerald was abrupt with the waitress, like he had to make something clear to her. Then he told a story.

"My father was a hereditary chief," he said. "Meetings were in our dad's kitchen, so as a kid I used to listen in. The Eurocan Pulp and Paper Mill was already operating, and we had stopped fishing oolichan because we smelled the taint." The Eurocan Pulp and Paper Mill operated in Kitimat for over 40 years before it closed in 2010. But Kitimat was a company town long before that, built in the 1950s by Alcan (the Aluminum Company of Canada), to take advantage of cheap hydro power.

"So this guy from the pulp mill came with his young

daughter to have tea in our kitchen. He said, 'I don't understand why you are all so afraid of the effluent from the mill. There's no taint. The effluent that is coming out of our pipe is so pure that you can drink it, thanks to the most modern technology.'"

Gerald shook his head.

"My dad never said anything," he continued. "He got up, went to the cupboard and took out two cups. He turned to the little girl, gave her a cup, helped her into her jacket and said, 'Let's go.' The man said, 'Where are you going?' My dad said, 'I know where the effluent pipe is. Let's go and your daughter can drink it and I'll drink it too.' The guy never moved."

Cecil leaned forward and said, "From my view, the politicians believe in industry, but they are destroying the industry of my people, the oolichan. The water they said you could drink actually destroyed the resources that the Creator has given us to feed us through the centuries. Now Enbridge says that the pipeline technology is safe."

"A lot of people don't understand how industrious our people really were," Gerald said. "On this river alone, we estimate that our people harvested 600 tonnes of oolichan in the springtime. This went on for untold generations. We've made our living here for thousands and thousands of years without destroying it."

Gerald got up to use the washroom, and Cecil leaned forward to get a better look at me.

"Can you turn off that tape recorder?"

I turned it off.

"Can you tell me why you are here?" he asked.

"I'm writing news stories about the pipeline because I'm worried about climate change," I said.

Then, for some reason, I started to cry. Cecil's kind gaze put me right into that part of my heart that sees how climate change is shredding the amazing, complex, abundant beauty of nature, not the nature that we visit in parks but the nature that sustains everything, all of us.

"My heart is breaking from the understanding of it," I said. "If I write about it, I don't feel so bad."

Cecil reached out a narrow hand with two fingers missing. He took mine.

"Thank you," he said as he patted my hand. "Now I will feel safe speaking with you."

"I was born in 1949," Gerald said. "So I grew up with Alcan. One of my first memories is lying on my grandmother's feather bed down by the river, where people lived for weeks at a time processing oolichan. Everybody had gone down to the river. I was nine, maybe ten years old. I lay there listening to this big humming noise—MMMMMMMMM—that I could hear clear from where I was. It was the first time I heard it, and I didn't know what it was."

It was the big fans of the aluminum factory pushing out the effluent into the river, the beginning of the end for the oolichan run. The oolichan once provided half of the Haisla's calories. Tainted oolichan would be like a stock market crash that destroyed half of the Haisla's wealth.

"At that time," Gerald said, "we didn't know what was going on."

"Remember the story about being told we could drink the effluent?" Cecil asked. "How close was that effluent pipe from the sea? It was very short, a mile or two contaminated and spoiled. Once you are past it, the water is still pure."

He indicated with a fork the idea of where the Kitimat effluent pipes might be, toward the bottom of the table.

"But the pipeline is like a snake, coming right into the headwaters of our river," Cecil said.

Across the top of the table came a spoon, the snake.

"If it breaks, the whole river is polluted. There's something here, only a few miles in from the ocean, telling us it's no good." Cecil indicated the Kitimat effluent pipe, the fork. "Are we going to listen to this? Before it started, the river was so good you could drink from it. Now, the river is dead."

After a pause he asked, "How do I get through to you, to people, what I have seen?"

"This is why we tell you the story of the oolichan," Gerald said. "There are some changes that people have to accept, but there are other changes that are so crazy. You don't pollute your own drinking water. A friend used to say our law is so simple: don't crap on your own dinner plate."

Enbridge has promised jobs from the pipeline, especially in Kitimat where the bitumen would be transferred from the pipeline and into supertankers. I asked Cecil if he trusted Enbridge's promise of jobs for his people.

"Trust is a very special word," Cecil said. He described residential school and how he became an alcoholic to hide the shame and pain of being treated like nothing. One day, words from his granny penetrated through his haze. She told him to go to where he was born, to the Kitlope.

"I went and sat there," Cecil said. "I began to change. I began to see what the government is doing to me and my people. How can they tell me I'm not human? I have a dream. I want to live in peace in the Creation I was given, to guard it against anyone who wants to bring it harm."

The West Fraser Timber Company wanted to log the Kitlope area. Officials told the Haisla that they could have 50 jobs and log the Kitlope themselves.

"I saw the young Haisla men and women out of work, and a tear came to my eye," Cecil said. "'Where are we going?' I asked myself. We are fighting something here that I don't understand."

The next morning, he got in his boat and went back to the place where he was born. There, he meditated.

"Then I understood," he said. "This money won't be there after they damage the river and the forest is gone. Once everything is destroyed, the industry will go too."

"I feel bad for so many unemployed," Cecil continued. "Look at all the homeless people all over Vancouver. I weep for them. But are we going to sacrifice something that will feed us for untold centuries? How do we make that decision? To have a stake now that will destroy the stake for our children? What benefit do we get from that trade?"

"We lose, I think," Cecil concluded.

Gerald agreed. "When it comes to the jobs angle, can anyone guarantee us when they shut the place down in 75 years what is it going to look like here? If there's an oil spill, it's all gone and where do we go? Right now, they're trucking in oolichan from the Nass River so we can make grease here because we don't have any of our own. If we have a spill here and we don't have any salmon left, are we going to truck that in too?"

He pointed to the blizzard out the window.

"Look out there. Up in the mountains, it's socked in. There's no way a human being can get in there and survive. If a pipeline burst in the headwaters of the Kitimat River or any rivers here where they're going to cross, there's absolutely no way they could get to it, no way they could fly a helicopter in this weather up to that site. How are they going to stop the flow? The spill they stopped cleaning up in Kalamazoo, Michigan, during the winter, that's flat, slow-moving water compared to our area."

Gerald wanted to get back to his wife in Kitimat Village. As we left the restaurant, I asked if I could take a picture of them.

"A picture of your new coat," Gerald teased Cecil.

They stood in the parking lot with snow swirling around them, tall and short. Then they got into the little sedan.

I trudged to the hotel office. The innkeeper seemed friendlier, like she knew I recognized her as part of my safety net. I said good-bye and hoisted my bag for another death-defying walk along snowbanks to a mall where I could catch a bus back to Terrace. As I felt her eyes on my back, I wondered if she saw the pipeline as a safety issue like I did. It reminded me of Gerald's comments about the people of Kitimat.

"I grew up here, and I saw prejudices against our people pretty early on," he said. "I thought, most of these people are pretty good people, what's happening here? Unless we start a new relationship in towns like this, big government is going to ram these projects down our throat. If we can't make progress in human relations here, then where else on Earth do we have a chance? If not now, when we know what we know about climate change and the other big issues that are happening around the world, when are we going to do it?"

He added, "Some people around here have really showed up on the pipeline issue. I have to say that I'm kind of optimistic right now."

CHAPTER EIGHT

Nectar

MY MOTHER became ill in the hospital that my father had helped to grow through several decades from a single building into a regional center. She was eighty-six, a widow for 19 years, and none of the doctors recognized her. I stalked them with a family photo from the year that our father was chief of staff. He steered a three-seated bicycle with my mom in the middle and five kids tucked here and there. I was the baby in the front basket. The doctors glanced at it, smiled and hurried away. Then Dr. Shukla arrived. He looked at the picture, gave a hearty chuckle and leaned down to my mother so that she could see his face.

"Mrs. Miller, remember that night when you and John had me over for dinner?" Dr. Shukla asked. "You served me fake champagne." He laughed at the memory of that fake champagne.

"Oh, yes, I do," she said. "Grapefruit juice and soda water." She gazed up at him from among the tubes, charm intact.

He turned to us, her children and grandchildren who had taken up residence in her hospital room with our bags of take-out burritos. A sense of royalty hung in the air, of someone who was owed everything.

"Your father was a very good friend to me when I was a new doctor here," Dr. Shukla said. "One night he invited me to dinner, and your mother served fake champagne." He laughed again.

"Finally," my sister said. "Someone who knows Mom."

We needed our mom to be known. She was the cheery, stubborn foundation on which all else was built, and she still ruled some of our most subterranean caverns. Now she presented us with a dilemma. Her pneumonia was worsening, and she had signed documents stating no artificial life support. But she didn't seem ready to die, and every day a new treatment appeared: oxygen, IV nutrition, breathing treatments in which her tiny body was shaken by an inflated vest. Sometimes she seemed like usual, other times she got confused.

We asked Dr. Shukla for advice. He described how his mother, when she was ninety, decided to drink only water from the Ganges River. Because it flows down from Mt. Everest, it is said to be so full of minerals that bacteria won't grow in it, and it can provide enough sustenance to live on for a month.

"My mother drank the holy water to prepare herself for death, and after ten days, she peacefully died," he said. "But your mother is receiving IV nutrition and oxygen, so you cannot take her home without them to die."

He shook his head. "Pneumonia brings a peaceful death, so it used to be called the 'old person's friend.' But now, we interfere."

The interference only drew things out. The pneumonia got the upper hand, and Mom was transferred to the extended care facility at her retirement home for comfort care. My sisters and brother left for their jobs, and I rode alone with her in the ambulance. I held one hand while she grasped the silky teddy that she had graciously accepted from a nurse with the other.

When we arrived at Regent's Point, we sat with her best friend Pat and her daughters, Pam and Judy, at a round table in the living room. My mother surveyed us and announced, "I feel human again."

She'd been allowed only ice chips in the hospital. A small stroke had impaired her ability to swallow, but now that we knew the pneumonia would win, that didn't matter. She dug into a little plastic cup of chocolate ice cream with a metal spoon and drilled through the rock-hard substance with surprising strength. I'd never seen her determination in such raw form. I wondered how much of it we had soaked up and rendered invisible as children.

After everyone left, I helped the nurses get Mom back into bed. Her hospital gown flapped open in the back, and I ran my hand over her thin, bumpy skin, her tiny bones. This delicate body was how I knew my mother. When she left it, what would I have of her?

As she slept, I laid my head on her belly, placed her hand on my head and cried. I did this a lot, after the others had left. It had given me a kinked neck. One day as I cried, I felt especially like a burning point in an expanse of grief. Why did I have to be so alone? My cell phone rang.

"Honey, I can't keep you out of my head," my friend Deena said. "What's going on?"

For ten minutes, she listened to me cry into the phone.

I spent nights in my mom's apartment, a five-minute walk from the nursing facility. One morning I came early to find her moving limb by limb toward the side of the bed like a sneaky starfish. I called the nurse to help me get her into the wheelchair that, for some reason, had no footrests. I had to wheel her backward so her dangling feet wouldn't catch the floor. We went to the table in the lounge, and I got her some more ice cream.

"Am I a vagrant now?" she asked. She struggled to keep her good posture and looked with disdain at the unfamiliar room.

I described each step that lead us to the nursing facility, how she went to the hospital for a test, they wanted her to stay, she had a small stroke, couldn't swallow well, got aspiration pneumonia and didn't pass the respiratory test that would allow the doctors to sedate her and insert a feeding tube.

"You decided to come here where you can do what you want," I said. "But the pneumonia is gaining on you. You'll probably die." If it was me, I'd want to know.

"That sounds about right," she said. "I have to think about this."

She knew how important it was, yet she was tired. Her head drooped, but she didn't want to return to bed. I worried that her spiritual needs weren't being met so I fetched her worn leather Bible from the bedside. Decades of penciled notes filled the margins. I started to read out loud from the Book of John. A woman in another wheelchair without footrests shuffled her chair along until she sat next to us. I looked at her. She looked away. I kept reading.

During the day, Pat and her daughters joined me at Mom's bedside. In the evenings, my brother Bill and his son Chase came. One evening, Mom decided to get up, and between all four of us, we managed it. Chase watched her struggle to stand up from her wheelchair. She couldn't do it, although she tried again and again. Later, I found him in tears in the hall.

"Why won't she just stop trying?" he asked.

She was falling like a broken bird into the chasm between her will to live and her failing body.

After everyone left and Mom was settled back in the bed, I held her hand and prayed. I wasn't a believer myself, but I appreciated the usefulness of a Great Third Person to whom I could say things that I would not say to her directly.

"Dear God," I said, "My mother has led a loving and useful life. Help her be proud, and satisfied with that. Help her know that her good influence will continue on in the people she helped and loved. Her spirit wants to live, but her body is dying. That puts us in a very difficult situation. Please help us get through this together, in a way that brings her satisfaction and peace. Amen."

"I am satisfied," my mom said. With tiny, wavering hands, she brought my head down to her lips for a good-night kiss.

"I love you," she said. Then she drifted into sleep.

"What are you hoping to get from spending this time with your mom?" Pat asked as we sat at the bedside. She was 80 and wore an enviable black leather jacket, coral lipstick and cat's-eyes sunglasses pushed up on her head. Her clear blue eyes waited, curious.

I immediately thought of several reasons to spend so much time at my mother's bedside: love, the huge backlog of gratitude that arose from an adult understanding of what she'd given me, my desire to know her in a deeper way, my inability to countenance the thought of her dying alone, my commitment to a stable climate that kept me from flying in and out, and I *could* be there. My work allowed it, and my husband, who loved Mom, wanted it. It even felt like a long overdue graduation from the status of "baby of the family" to an authoritative adult who applied nursing and law experience to get the best care for our mom.

But Pat's penetrating gaze looked deeper. So I groped around and found a sense that we find meaning when we reach for the experiences we evolved with as a species, the experiences that have always been a part of human existence.

"I don't think modern life works for me at the level of my deep emotions," I said. "Important stages in developing as a person can get glossed over when they seem sad and uncomfortable. I want to live to the full capacity that evolution gave me because I think that will be the most satisfying life, even if it means feeling more grief. Maybe it will develop my under-standing as a human."

Pat smiled at me and nodded.

Every day, Pat, her daughters and I continued our quiet conversation around my mom's bed. She rarely woke up. We greeted her friends, who started to show up as soon as my sib-lings left. They were surprised to see me there, the aloof black sheep of my mother's daughters. For decades, I avoided every-one associated with the church of my youth. Now all that meant nothing. I wanted to hear their stories: how she took care of a little boy once a week so his mother could manage better; how, for decades, she warmly greeted each church-goer at the sanctuary door with her elegant clothes and her lovely smile; her recent visits to lonely people at her retirement home.

"I don't think you have any idea about your mom," Pam, Pat's elder daughter, said. "I was bedridden for two years, and she visited me several times a week to keep me company."

Pam was right. I hadn't known that. To me, Pam was the daughter of my mom's best friend and a busy, successful busi-ness woman. I had wondered why she took so much time from work to sit with my mother and me.

Other friends said they went to my mom for advice. Each received a variation of the same wisdom: in difficult situations, leave judgments behind and think about what you can do that will make things better.

After a week, Mom stopped waking up. One day a huge cushioned wheelchair that could be made flat like a bed ap-peared in the room. I wrapped her in blankets and took her out to the small courtyard. We could hear the birds, and the breeze blew around us. Dehydration gave her face a narrow, triangu-lar look with giant ears, like an elf. I noticed that her toe nails were still sparkly pink from when we got pedicures together three months earlier. I remembered her reaction to my choice of polish, blood red.

"That's a statement," she observed, "but I can't tell what it means."

When I felt her feet and hands, she seemed warm, plenty warm in fact. Her friends came by, pleased to spend time in the pretty courtyard. I played classical music on my computer and read them stories from my mom's childhood that I had transcribed over the years.

After we got her back to bed, I left for the yoga class that kept me going. As I walked through the gates of her retirement community, my cell phone rang. A nurse was on the other end.

"Your mother has a temperature," she said. "It's a serious situation."

I headed back to Mom's bedside, where the nurse fanned her with a sheet. Pat was still there.

"I think I overheated Mom in the courtyard," I whispered.

Pat shook her head.

"Don't you hang on to that," she whispered back. "We all needed to be outside."

By the next morning, Mom's breathing was ragged, several breaths together followed by a long silence. All day, the intervals between breaths grew longer. I texted my husband, "Did your mom have long periods of no breath before she died?"

"Yes, on the last day," he texted back. I felt him there, understanding.

So that's where we were. The last day. I'd been living this strange life for over two weeks, yet now it seemed so abrupt.

Pat, her daughters and I spent the day holding Mom's hands and rubbing her feet. In the evening, I was alone with her. I took her hand and watched her breathe, six breathes, pause, eight breathes, pause.

I had read from the Book of John every day, and only one page of dense print remained. It was the time of day I usually read to her. I had a strong feeling that if I started, she would die before I finished, yet it was time to begin. After ten minutes, when I reached the last chapter, her breath stopped. I looked up from her Bible. She took one more breath. That was all. I kept hold of her hand.

Slowly, a sense of sweetness filled the room. Maybe it drifted from her body. It flowed around me and, with each breath, into me.

The door opened behind me. My brother Bill stood at my side.

"I can't believe it," he said, taking it in. "I had to stop at every traffic light."

I stood up and opened the window to allow her spirit egress, something I'd read about in old books.

"Let's just sit," I said. Bill pulled up a chair, and I returned my attention to the sweet suffusion that drifted through the air.

Maybe when you love someone, I thought, you are preparing for a moment that you don't even realize will come. If you are ready, the distilled essence of the loved one can enter you like nectar. Maybe it finds the similar substance within you and awakens it. You feel both your own awakened self and the beloved within you.

For decades, I had balanced all my prickly convictions with the desire to be a good daughter, but we had seemed so different. I was an overweight feminist professional woman and then a grubby farmer. She was a svelte and stylish homemaker, church leader and adventurous partner to a strong-willed man. In her later years, she travelled the world while I refused to fly. When she visited our homestead, she wore white clothes that excluded her from all the soil-based activities that I found satisfying. She chose sparkly pink polish, and I, at my only pedicure, chose blood red.

Now, finally, I had managed to purify my love for her into something that both looked after her needs and clarified my own spirit. I could feel her essence crystallizing around my love for her. It seemed natural and inevitable that we would find each other in this way. Perhaps that was what we had longed for, beneath our differences, for all those years.

CHAPTER NINE

Falling into Place

"AN ANCIENT HUMAN jawbone was found next to our new house," Barry said over the phone. "You can tell it is ancient because the teeth are flat. They look like they were filed down from chewing something hard."

"A human jawbone?" I repeated. The words made no sense to me.

"There's a stop work order on the whole property," he added.

My mother had died the day before. Nothing sank in, and much had stormed away. I hadn't been able to recall my voice-mail password for two weeks. I misplaced my passport. I lost the keys to a safety deposit box with my mom's jewellery.

"Things will come back to you," Pat told me. "It's part of grief."

Barry's news was difficult to comprehend. Death, an infrequent visitor in my life, was knocking on two doors at once. The jawbone settled alongside my mother's death in a shadowy canyon away from the surface of life.

At that surface church programs, from the memorial services of family friends who had died, cluttered the floor on which I sat—my high-school math teacher, my kindergarten friend's mother, a few people my age. Each program took me back to old memories and, more practically, gave clues about the decisions we needed to make about prayers, soloists, ministers, charities, fonts, photos and so on.

"Listen, don't worry about it," my husband said into my silence. "It doesn't matter right now. I have to find an archaeologist. I'll hire the guy who reported the jawbone to the provincial government. He's local."

After living on our Cortes Island homestead for 14 years, my family moved to the city so my son could go to high school there. We decided to build a smaller house for when we moved back, on land we had purchased with friends. The new house site overlooks Desolation Sound. Midden, a deposit of ancient clam shells, forms the bank down to the water. We saw the midden as an ancient seal of good housekeeping, the compost of hundreds, or maybe thousands, of years of inhabitants. Like us, these people must have chosen this place for its view of Vancouver Island to the south, a part-time stream close by and a clam beach below. We buried a septic tank in front of the house to keep the shoreline waters pristine and built the house well back from the midden bank on the pale brown forest soils.

Our friends Iris and Volker were building the new house. Volker carved massive beams with beautiful images of ferns and wild mushrooms. A yellow cedar drift log post revealed the spiralling structure of the tree. After three years, the house was exquisitely artful. But it had taken twice as long as planned and still wasn't finished.

No power at the house site slowed Iris and Volker's progress. They had to use hand tools or a generator. Power was supposed to be on the way. After six years, our group of land partners managed to finance an underground power cable to be buried along the kilometer of road. We paid the contractors up front to dig the trench and lay the cable. Barry and I were on the well driller's schedule. When we returned to Cortes for the summer, the house would be unfinished but at least we'd have electricity and water.

And then, Volker found the human jawbone.

In California, alone in my mother's apartment, I curled up on her guest bed and relived the free fall of her last two weeks of life. Helping her to a good death felt like landing a 747 without a pilot's license. I felt shaken and sad, and very relieved.

My short biography for the funeral program started with her birth in Puyallap, Washington, the daffodil capital of the world, a hieroglyph of her cheerful nature and fortunate circumstances. It ended with a quote from a report one of my nephews wrote in grade five: "Elie always tries to see the best in people and situations. These are her words of advice and love."

Every few hours, I was scoured by child-woman tears of longing for the way she used to snuggle me in bed as I recited multiplication tables and her gracious curiosity about my mystifying choices.

"Now tell me about that interesting sweater," she might say regarding a thrift store find. Or, "Now tell me why you want to move to Canada."

Even so, between the funeral arrangements and the floods of grief, I had time on my hands. I talked to Barry a lot. He wasn't sleeping at night. The provincial government's requirements regarding the jawbone made no sense.

"It's Kafka-esque," he said. "I think we just have to pay for whatever the archaeologist wants to do. It lacks parameters."

I told him I could be the point person for a while, if he wanted.

"It's not that big of a deal," the provincial archaeologist reassured me. "We try to be reasonable. We can expedite your case. Should be up and going in a few weeks."

It was only April. We'd still have power and water by summer.

The provincial archaeologist agreed that we could quickly clear the power cable route of archaeological significance because it was far from the shoreline midden. The local archaeologist, the one who reported the jawbone, would have a look, file a report, and the trenching could go forward as planned.

A month later, the local archaeologist sent us his preliminary report. It stated that the trench would have "severe impacts" on an area of "high archaeological significance." He included pictures of things he had found partway up the road and far from the shoreline midden: a broken rock, a piece of slate, a smooth beach cobble and a burnt bone.

"These are not what I think of as artifacts," I said to Barry as we read the report. "There's no arrowheads or chisels or even any worked rock."

July came, with no power line and no well. A propane stove on the deck of our unfinished house was my kitchen. To do dishes, I poured warm water on my plate and scrubbed it with a pine cone. The water was clean enough to dump beneath a tree.

Other times, I took the dishes in a basket down the steep dirt path to the seashore and scrubbed them with seaweed. Tiny crabs threatened me with lifted pincers and then bounced around grabbing bits of food.

Our sixteen-year-old son, faced with two months without showers, electricity or Wi-Fi, immediately decamped to a friend's house. He stopped by every few days for dinner. I was unhappy about his absence, about a summer of camping in an unfinished house and that we hadn't had a real home on Cortes for three years and I couldn't invite my family to visit. I was particularly unhappy with the local archaeologist. I showed his report to local artifact hobbyists. No one thought the items pictured in his report qualified as artifacts.

We hired a new archaeologist. But the report had gone to the provincial government, so we had to apply for a Site Alteration Permit. This required consultation and approval by the three First Nations whose traditional territory overlaps in that area. The provincial archaeologist no longer talked about expediting our permit.

As I sipped my tea in a camp chair on the deck, the sea below sounded like the breath of a gentle beast. Oystercatchers piped up now and then as they flew from spot to spot along the shore in their endless search for clams. Much further out, Mitlenatch Island held a pale golden glow. I wasn't fooled by its peaceful aspect, because I had kayaked into the mayhem of thousands of nesting gulls scolding the eagles, crows and terns that circled above, hungry for eggs and spotty-headed chicks. Mitlenatch Island reflected the feelings in my heart, peaceful from a distance as I watched the water and sipped my tea but, on closer approach, full of squawking birds.

I had avoided Iris and Volker since the stop work order. One morning, Iris left a loaf of fresh baked bread on our doorstep, with a small jar of rough red salt. I saw her and Volker that night at a community event. Afterward, we rode our bikes home together. I told them I'd like to talk to them about the jawbone.

"Yes," said Volker. "Let's turn this thing around."

We planned a visit for the next day.

The next morning, I walked the old logging road through the forest to the Loon Ranch where Iris's family and her parents, Hannes and Brigitte, have lived since emigrating from Germany in 1980. Volker and I sat in Iris's kitchen where everything is made of big pieces of carved wood. Volker is an excitable man, fiftyish, with green eyes and a strong build. Iris kept busy in the background. She's tremendously tall with wide blue eyes and hair that goes curly or frizzy, depending on the weather.

"The first piece of wood we walked to the back, I saw it," Volker told me.

The path from the deck to the storage shed at the back went over a drainage pipe to the septic tank that had been covered with soil from the midden below.

"I saw it, but I didn't clue in," Volker continued. "I just accidently noticed. And then the second walk by, I look at this closer, and it looked like nothing I have seen, and I picked it up and knew right away: *VOW*, this is human."

Volker uses this Germanic "Wow" a lot. The sound drops, like a heavy rock. His friends say it too, because it's fun. *VOW*.

"I looked at the teeth and, *vow*, I've never seen teeth like this. They were worked, like somebody filed them or something. It had only half its teeth, but they were super-healthy teeth. Someone said they work the hide with these teeth, or the grit from clams grinds them down. The jawbone was small. I think it is the jawbone of a woman. We looked around for more bones or teeth. But there was nothing else."

Iris took the jawbone home at lunchtime. Volker stopped in to watch the Chelsea-Barcelona soccer game at Hannes' on his way home.

"This guy Jeff who plays soccer sometimes was there," he said. "Hannes barely knows him; he invited himself over. I told

Jeff about the jawbone, and it turns out he's an archaeologist, and he asked me to show him where it came from, so I did. He looked around your house site and said, 'Yes, of course, there is midden all over the place.'"

"He came back that night and said we had done the right thing. I said, 'What are you talking about? What right thing?' I was just writing Barry to tell him about the jawbone. Jeff said he had reported the jawbone to the provincial government because that was his professional duty and we had done the right thing. I said to him, 'Why are you already jumping on the thing?' The next I know the police come by to collect the jawbone because it was a human being, and they said to me they had to take it."

I later told this sequence of events to a friend who had closely followed our house project over the last three years and, every few months, complimented us on our patience. Her eyes widened when I told her how an archaeologist invited himself to Hannes' on the same day that the jawbone was found and Volker stopped by to watch soccer, and how that was the same day my mother died.

"Honey, you can't *make* this stuff up!" she said.

One aspect of having a jawbone found on our land was the edgy feeling it gave me for having broken the taboo against disturbing human remains. I couldn't sleep well for the first few nights there. Barry didn't share my discomfort.

"People have lived and died just about everywhere," he remarked. "Soil is made from the bodies of creatures and plants that came before us."

Another aspect was how the jawbone brought home the fact that we are on land that was occupied by First Nations for thousands of years, land to which they have unextinguished rights because they never signed treaties giving it away. Even without disturbing human remains, I've always felt like a taker in my relationships to First Nations people.

Our house site is in the traditional territory of the Sliammon, the Klahoose and the Holmolco First Nations, each of which would need to approve the Site Alteration Permit. The Klahoose First Nation has its main reserve on the island, so I called the councillor I know there. She's very composed by nature, and I'm so eager that I feel like a hummingbird who is tolerated by an enigmatic bear. When I visited her in her office, she didn't seem too thrilled about the situation.

"The RCMP came by my house and tried to give me the jawbone," she said. "I told them, no thank you. I don't want it lying around while I try to figure out what to do with it."

She said they would rebury it on either the Klahoose or Sliammon reserve.

I asked her if she knew how our house site was used in the past. She waved to a file cabinet of archaeology reports.

"We don't make this information available," she said. "It's for use in treaty negotiations."

I asked if we could get the jawbone carbon-dated. Shell midden preserves bones, and this one could be 200 years old, it could be 9,000 years old. I was pretty damn curious.

"I think these remains have been through enough already," she said.

I wanted to imagine the life of the ancient woman whose jawbone we had found, so I asked around about how our house site was used before contact with Europeans.

Our new archaeologist didn't think people lived at our house site at all.

"This seems to be a secondary deposit," he said. "Your bank is too high for a First Nations village site, but the adjacent cove is perfect. The early loggers probably scooped the midden from there and dumped it at your house site so their machines wouldn't get mired."

The Klahoose archaeology specialist didn't know anything specific to the house site. He said that the adjacent cove that looks both north and south was a watching place. Families took turns camping there, watching for traders and raiders. A family member would run to the main village if there was news.

Volker said one native friend told him the house site was a Sliammon slave camp, but he thought it was a year-round village.

"The salmon used to come right up onto the shore," Volker said, "and the herring laid eggs on the eel grass just out there. *VOW*, what a place for food."

The Klahoose elder I spoke with had no knowledge of our house site. He had spent his childhood in residential school until he ran away to Seattle to escape the provincial government's jurisdiction.

"We're still trying to piece it all back together," he said.

Eventually, it occurred to Barry and me that a jawbone far from its skeleton is a lonely thing. I left a message for my Klahoose friend, inviting the Klahoose to bury the jawbone back at our house site. After a few weeks, she responded that they planned to repatriate the jawbone on our land with a traditional ceremony.

A bluff behind our house has six cement statues, busts of women staring out to sea, tucked next to rock outcrops and under arbutus trees. You might not notice them unless you wander off the trail. But if you do, you might return for their eerie beauty. They are all portraits of Brigitte, the matriarch of the Loon Ranch next door, made by different hands at a portrait workshop Volker once taught.

Next to the bluff, a popular beach trail descends to a sandy cove. Our land partnership covenanted the trail for public use and named it Brigitte's Beach. Barry and I went one night to tell Brigitte the news. She and Hannes were playing solitaire at their kitchen nook, each with a separate deck of tiny, ornate cards. Brigitte has a round face and clear blue eyes. When Barry and I told her about the name, she raised her hands in the air and let them drop back to her lap. Then she beamed. In the silence, her tall and wiry husband Hannes said, "Finally."

We felt as if we had dropped by with the last piece to an important puzzle.

My husband and son returned to the city in early September while I waited for the traditional ceremony to repatriate the jawbone. My Klahoose friend told me the jawbone would be buried in a handmade box.

For ten days, I was mostly alone, and I found myself talking to the ancient woman of the jawbone. Who were you? I asked. Slave? Villager? Watcher? I imagined her chewing deer skin to make it soft enough for baby shoes as she stared out toward Mitlenatch Island. Every now and then, she rearranged the clams that were drying on a stone hearth.

I thought I might dream about her, but I didn't. Instead I dreamt about my mother's last days in the hospital. I regretted that I hadn't crawled into her bed, through the IVs and monitors, to hold her. I regretted that I hadn't helped her to get up all those times she wanted to, even though the nurses had asked us not to. In my dream, I spooned her in her bed and helped her up every time she asked.

Most days through the summer, I worked in the orchard at our old homestead, cutting back the encroaching blackberries and alders. I hacked away until my arms tingled and burned at night and I couldn't sleep. It was time to pick fruit anyway. I cut up peaches for the food drier at the foot of the peach tree and filled my basket with blackberries. Every year for over a decade, I have made blackberry cordial for my mom.

"My friends love it over vanilla ice cream," she said. "It's such a simple, elegant dessert."

I couldn't stop myself. I bought the vodka and sugar, and started the cordial.

In the evenings, I sat quietly on the bluff with Brigitte's statues. I felt satisfied that we had connected Brigitte's name to that place. Somehow, it brought my mom closer to our new house. My mom and Brigitte were born the same year. Neither of them were public heroes, but they both lived useful, purposeful lives. They helped take care of needs in the larger world. Brigitte ran a home for vulnerable children in Germany. My mom raised five children and volunteered a lot of time to her church. I admired them both and hoped my life would prove so clearly useful.

I imagined the woman of the ancient jawbone telling me that the beach name gave Brigitte the satisfaction of knowing her name would be on people's lips for many years to come, and it also recognized how we all just pass through these places that we love. I told her that I wished I could name the place for her as well, for all of us, to say to those who would follow, "We were here. We loved this place too. We loved it very much."

The ancient woman pointed out that Brigitte's name is a goddess name, the keeper of the hearth. The beach is named for all of us, hearth keepers and sea watchers.

I drove my truck out to the main road on the day of the ceremony. Mary Clare, one of our land partners, met me. She's an island Amazon, tall and big-boned, who works as a paramedic, sells pottery and apples, tends a garden and orchard and helps raise sheep, her child and sometimes other people's children as well.

The contractor also appeared, in a pickup truck with giant tires. He had dug a half kilometer of open trenches in which to place the power line along the side of the road when the archaeologist was present, and then he disappeared for a month. A dump truck full of sand followed him, then a flatbed full of cable conduit. The contractor told me that he would block the road to our house.

Why did he reappear on the day of the ceremony? I wondered. Maybe it was a sign that the ceremony was already melting the mysterious obstacles that kept the new house and power line project from completion. On the other hand, maybe it was just another instance of unfortunate timing, of things gone wrong. Either way, I didn't want to send the contractor away. I ran to ask Hannes if the elders could drive through the Loon Ranch.

About twenty minutes later, my Klahoose friend showed up with four women in her truck. They joked while we waited for the others to arrive.

"I like my salmon fresh, silver and all the same size so they hang just right in the smoke house," my friend said.

"OCD," said one of the other women, and they all laughed.

Eventually, four trucks of Klahoose and Sliammon members waited in the road. We drove slowly under ancient apple trees, through the grey rickety gate behind Hannes and Brigitte's house to the forest and down the steep hill to our house. People wandered around and admired the view of the ocean through the trees. They shivered in the shade, so I piled jackets and sweaters on the deck, and they put them on.

The Sliammon elder who performs such ceremonies, a woman in her mid-sixties, chose a burying place directly below the house between two big Douglas firs. Another Sliammon elder, a man with long hair, built the ceremonial fire just above it. He placed cedar kindling in an elaborate rectangular lattice. Someone placed two cardboard boxes covered with napkins on the deck. They held the ceremonial food that had been pre-pared the day before to feed the ancestors.

I told the female elder that my mom died the day the jaw-bone was found, and so the jawbone and my mom were mixed together in my mind.

"I miss her so much, and I am trying to learn how to have a relationship with someone after they die," I said.

"They are always with us," she said. "They are here in this place now, and they will always be with us. When I am feeling out of sorts or as if things are not quite right, I build a fire and feed the ancestors because it reminds me how meaningful it is to be here."

As the ceremony began, elders gave us each a cedar bough to hold for protection. The Klahoose chief handed down a small handmade box to the men who had dug the hole. They placed it in the earth and covered it while an elder drummed and sang a song.

The elder leading the ceremony placed the cardboard boxes of food on the scaffold of kindling and nestled four plastic bot-tles of tea close by. The fire was lit. She asked us to turn away.

"Otherwise, it is like asking someone to a feast and then staring at them while they eat alone," she said.

She said that it was a good time to ask for blessings for our-selves, our families, the people of this place and for the place itself. I imagined each person in my family, and my extended clan and the land partners. I thought about how we chose this place to live out the rest of our lives, watching the oystercatchers and listening to the slap of the seals. I tried not to worry about the elders feeling cold, or when to light the propane stove for tea. The excavator clanked in the background.

After about ten minutes, as the smoke still wafted around us, the elder suggested that we could be swept with cedar boughs if we wanted to be cleansed that way.

My turn came to step between the two elders holding cedar branches. One of the men whispered as he brushed me, "Thank you for having us to your land and for recognizing us and honoring us. It means a lot to our people." My guilty intruder wanted to protest that no, I was in his debt, but his graciousness prevented me. I smiled and nodded to him.

After we had all been swept, the chief thanked everyone who participated in the events leading up to the ceremony: the person who found the jawbone, the archaeologist who reported it, the contractors who are working on the job, the landowners, myself, the counsellor who organized the ceremony and the Sliammon people who came all the way from Powell River by boat.

I'd noticed at other Klahoose events that *everyone* gets thanked, even those whose contributions were a mixed bag. Maybe living with the same people for generations teaches the benefit of memorializing positive contributions while letting the negative ones drop away. It reminded me of my mom's words of advice, to move forward without judgments.

"This has been a good day," the chief concluded. "Let us share it with others in our words."

I asked to speak. During the nights I laid awake with burning arms, I had prepared a complicated speech that ranged from First Nations rights to my mom's life and death. Instead, I said, "Thank you so much for being here. It is an honor to have your blessing on the land and an honor to be in your traditional territory."

People shifted into a more relaxed way. I felt glad I'd left aside any mention of my sense of intrusion; it wasn't about me. It was about a culture's participation in a place since time immemorial, and how that culture lives on in ways I couldn't fully understand. I felt like a piece of driftwood that complimented the trees on their roots.

Afterward, I thanked the woman elder for the ceremony.

"It all has so much meaning," she said.

I tried to describe an idea I'd come up with one evening as I stared out to sea from the deck. That view and those sounds had shaped my thoughts all summer long. The living blue sea, the smudge of Mitlenatch Island, the seal slap and the oystercatchers' shrieks were imprinted on my mind. The woman of the ancient jawbone and her people may have experienced the same influences and imprints. I suggested that perhaps that made the woman of the ancient jawbone a common ancestor. I shared her land influences; the Klahoose and Sliammon people shared her genes.

The elder just smiled.

The trucks drove off, but I wasn't ready for the ceremony to end.

"I'd like to offer my mom some blackberry cordial," I told Mary Clare.

"My mother would like some cordial too," she replied.

She rebuilt the fire, and I decanted cordial, black with sunshine, into glasses. Warmth finally flooded in between the gap in the trees. We poured cordial onto the flames for our mothers. Rather than turning away from their feast, we politely joined them with a bit of Scotch and talked Moms.

Her mother, like mine, was a woman of faith who believed in the importance of a useful, purposeful life. She loved to sing and had times of depression later in her life.

I told Mary Clare about how my mom and her 20 friends, known as the "Walky Talkies," disappeared into the desert every year and left bewildered children to eat their fathers' pancakes. Once, the Walky Talkies filmed a Western in costumes from their kids' dress-up bins. No one outside the group ever saw that movie, but we saw photos of our moms dressed as damsels, horses and villains, laughing harder than they ever laughed at home.

My pride in my mother's sense of fun surprised me.

Pema Chodron, a Buddhist nun, wrote that self-improvement is a subtle aggression against oneself; the kindest thing to do is to befriend who you already are. Maybe usefulness was a form of self-improvement.

"Maybe our moms felt like they had to pay for their existence by being useful," I said. "But maybe in fact existence is a gift."

I'd been to a public hearing in which a First Nations woman testified about the significance of her traditional territory.

"This land is my school," she said. "It is where my granny taught me to honor the day."

"To honor the day"—that stayed with me.

Her protection of her traditional territory wasn't rooted in a desire to be useful. It flowed from honoring its gifts on a particular day.

Mary Clare and I fell quiet. The sun gained warmth. A seal slapped the water below, and oystercatchers squawked along the beach. We raised our glasses.

I made a Greek salad that evening and took it to Volker's. Iris was away on a hiking trip. Volker was eating soup. We shared food, and I told him about the ceremony.

"So we are happy now?" he asked. "We are friends?"

"We're happy, we're friends." I said. "We will have a party to recognize the amazing house you built, once we have water and electricity."

On my last evening, I poured the final splash from the bottle of Glenlivet, sat down in my deck chair and looked out at the sea. Lingering light made the mountains of Vancouver Island dark and purple. Mitlenatch Island, a thin black line, snuggled beneath. The ocean merged the pink-and-blue sky into a plate of lavender light.

The Scotch tasted hot and stiff, so I added water. The next sip flooded sweet heat across my tongue. It reminded me of how the ceremony for the ancestor helped me to taste the present, to know that I am just one of the many who have received the gift of a limited time in this beautiful place. I shared the place, with the woman of the ancient jawbone among others.

The Sliammon elder believed that all those people were present with me now. I thought about Brigitte's statues standing sentinel on the bluff behind the house and the jawbone nestled beneath the tree below me. I thought of my mother and the nectar I had assimilated after her last breath. Now the people who had been in this place before added meaning to my presence, and I could continue their meaning as well. I felt in good company, among tenders of the hearth and watchers of the sea.

CHAPTER TEN

Journey to Numen Land

I FLOAT ABOVE a grassy hill, adjusting my altitude by the depth of my breath.

I sit cross-legged on the sandy bottom of a light-blue sea, watching dolphins swim past high above me.

A resplendent quetzal lands on my head. It ruffles its brilliant tail feathers down the back of my neck as it settles in.

I don't pursue these experiences; they just occur. Anything can happen in Numen Land.

In Latin, *Numen* means "a nod of the head," a god's head to be precise, a divine thumbs-up. In English, "numen" means "divine power." Rudolph Otto, an influential German theologian, coined the term "numinous" to describe intense experiences that seem to arise from the "wholly other," experiences that are mysterious, terrifying and fascinating. Carl Jung, the 20th century psychiatrist, described some aspects of the unconscious as numinous—"unconditional, dangerous, taboo, magical."

Last winter, I decided to make Numen Land my travel destination. I sought what travelers generally seek when they leave home: new experiences and a deeper understanding. Flying to India—a typical numinous experience for travellers—might have provided those things, but it would also emit 7.75 tonnes of greenhouse gases. That's three to five times the amount a single person would emit each year if we all agreed to equal responsibility for keeping the climate safe. And so I decided to try to reach Numen Land in dreams, from my own bed. In this way, I would avoid air travel's inherent contradiction, the way it simultaneously teaches us to love the world and at the same time hurts it.

Among Numen Land's obscure advantages is its close fit with my theory that fulfilment lies in the activities that evolution designed us for, such as sleep. Theoretically, sleep occupies a third of our lives, but not many people get the full eight hours anymore. Before artificial lighting, people got even more. Europeans slept for a few hours, woke up for a while, then slept some more before morning. They stayed in bed during their awake time and, according to historic accounts, read, prayed and meditated on their dreams. As I prepared for my own voyage to Numen Land, I imagined that drowsy interval as a liminal time, an enlightening suffusion between consciousness and numen, like oil and water tumbled in a jar.

It turns out that sleep has political implications as well. Jonathon Crary, an art historian at Columbia University, criticizes how our culture sees sleep as an activity for losers because it is economically useless. It's a time-out from the neo-liberal paradigm in which we all to want to spend every last minute pursuing our individual needs and desires in a world where everything is available 24/7. Sleep's cyclical patterns aren't compatible with "the deathliness of all the accumulation, financialization, and waste that have devastated anything once held in common."

Crary's ideas confirmed that my plan to sleep a lot wasn't lazy. It was radical. It pushed back on a devastating economy. I felt slightly heroic, but not totally immune to the way my friends glanced away when I told them my winter plan was to get a lot of sleep. As if I was being dull. So I dropped it and listened to tales of their great times in faraway places. I asked questions like an abstemious diabetic inquiring about whether the chocolate frosting is buttercream or ganache. Happiness for my friends' interesting lives tumbled in my heart with awareness of our demographics: that our incomes of over $40,000 a year put us in the world's wealthiest 8 percent that is responsible for 50 percent of all greenhouse gases.

The first morning I woke up with one foot still in Numen Land.

My dreams slipped back into my unconscious mind like filings pulled by a magnet. I had placed a pen and pad by my bed, but I had already forgotten the end of my dream by the time I scrawled the first part.

The following few mornings, I rushed to the computer with my numen. I typed whatever I remembered: cooking a chicken at the top of a cliff in a Bolivian marketplace; cooking chicken for everyone at my neighbor's house; sliding a turkey through butter I spilled on a countertop. I found mysterious patterns in my dreams—such as a propensity for cooking poultry.

However, some dreams seemed obvious enough. One night, after a lot of intense emotion, I dreamed the ocean flooded. Another night, I shopped for clothes, and it was like shopping for a new persona: I exchanged a pair of black high-heeled pumps for new swim fins.

But most of my dreams felt mundane. I went here and there, with a companion or without, into buildings full of people, some of whom I knew or once knew, some of whom I'd never met.

More and more, my attempt to reach the numinous in my dreams made me feel like a tourist eating at McDonald's in

Kolkata, when what I wanted was to meditate in an ashram in the Himalayas.

I decided to visit a Jungian analyst to help me find more meaning in my dreams.

Jung viewed dreams as the bridge between the conscious and unconscious minds, an expression of both personal material and archetypes from a "collective unconscious" that consists of core human experiences. Jung's most important archetype, the Self, consists of the conscious and unconscious minds working together toward psychological wholeness. Maybe a Jungian analyst could guide me to this deeper territory.

My analyst worked out of her apartment. She greeted me at the top of the staircase, an older woman with puffy grey hair and a cotton sweater printed with spirals, arrows and ungulates, like the figures painted in ancient caves. She was bulky up top in a healthy way, like Jung himself. I settled into a rattan chair with my paper full of random dreams, and I asked her what I might expect from this analysis.

"A sense of belonging and wholeness," she said.

"My dreams just patter about," I complained. "They seem like nonsense."

"By asking questions," she said, "you tell the dream maker what you want to know. Keep watching. Your dreams might surprise you."

"Is the collective unconscious like God, all powerful and wise?" I asked.

She gave me a long look.

"It's more like nature," she said gently, "red in tooth and claw."

She continued on. "Daily experiences provide the vocabulary which the dream maker combines into the message needed by the conscious mind. The message usually pertains to finding a middle way: if you are sad, you might have happy dreams. Or dream images may combine opposites."

"I had a dream about dogs," I said. "A yellow lab and a black lab running around."

"Dogs represent your instinctual self or your body," she said. "Those contrasting colors can indicate opposites, a tendency to polarize toward joy or despair. The dream maker seeks a middle way, like combining opposing tendencies into something more workable."

I do swing from joy to despair, and it interested me that it might be an inherent tendency of my body. That week a yellow lab and a black lab tore past me in the park. Then it happened a second time, a different pair of labs, one yellow and one black, with a different owner. I found it odd, given my dream, but decided I just hadn't been attuned to dogs like this in the past. Then a pair of terriers, one yellow and one black, trotted by. The next week I told the analyst about the dogs.

"Jung would call that synchronicity," she said. "When you start to pay attention, meaningful events occur. They aren't causally connected, but they reflect an underlying dynamic that governs human experience."

With this intriguing thought, I redoubled my dream efforts: eight, even nine hours and requests to the dream maker as I drifted off: more dolphins, please. And fewer motorized park benches that can't be steered.

Slowly but surely, I noticed that my dreams had started to fill in what I longed for in waking life. When I missed my sisters and brothers, I dreamed of families sitting around in their living room hanging out. When I missed my mom, I found her frozen in a snowbank and revived her in a cottage by a blazing fire. Then we had tea and chatted.

One morning on awakening, a bubble of numen floated up from the unconscious, the attractive stuff, not the fear and trembling. It burst with warmth and comfort in the depths of my chest, a potent fragment of an immense and positive actuality, some bigger field underlying my conscious mind.

But the numen didn't appear in quantity until I got desperate.

One day, my son told Barry that he had a big bony lump on the back of his ankle.

"It hurts when I play soccer," he said.

He lifted his pant leg. A hard protrusion of several inches reached from his heel to the bottom of his calf.

Our family doctor sent him directly to the orthopedic doctor who sent him directly to the cancer specialist which, in Canada, took three weeks. This gave me plenty of time to study osteosarcoma malignancies on the Web and marinate myself in terror. It didn't help that my son felt irritated by my intense reactions to things, the way I jumped when someone walked into the room or gasped when he was driving and a car's brake lights went on up ahead. He was spending more and more time in his room, appearing only at dinner.

Barry and I went to the new *Hunger Games* movie for distraction, the last two seats, front row. The screen loomed over us as huge figures threatened, whipped and killed each other. I made three trips to the washroom to avoid the stimulation and then sank into my seat and tuned out. My thoughts drifted toward my son. All would be fine. The odds that he had bone cancer were so small. Cancer couldn't forcibly abduct us from normal society. But what about Terry Fox, who had osteosarcoma and bravely ran across Canada on an artificial leg before dying? He didn't foresee a future defined by cancer. Who did? Yet it happened. Our family hovered between two completely different futures, one of them dominated by illness and fear of death. I laid my head on the warmth of Barry's shoulder. A few tears squeezed out, then more, until I sobbed. Giant waves sloshed across the screen and threatened to drown everyone.

"Let's get out of here," Barry whispered. We stumbled from the theatre, our cancer adrenaline soaked in movie adrenaline.

My son kept his bedroom door closed. When he came down for dinner, I wanted to touch him and hold him. Instead, we sat on stools at the kitchen counter and silently spooned butter chicken from the electric pan onto beds of brown rice, while I tried to think about anything but cancer. My heart panged with longing for reconciliation.

That night as I drifted to sleep I grieved his aloofness. It made me wonder how it must have felt for my father to die with me, his youngest daughter, so aloof and unreconciled. The distance between us began to grow when I was thirteen with my announcement that I would no longer attend church.

"I'm old enough to take care of my own spiritual life," I said. "Six hours a week with a bunch of hypocrites isn't part of it."

"You will go to church until you leave this house," he said. "If you don't believe, you are damned to go to hell."

I ran from the kitchen in tears, convinced he had chosen his god, an apparition, over me, his daughter.

He died of a heart attack at seventy-four, jogging up a hill, still a doctor, still in control. I was thirty-five at the time. As I lay in bed, I thought about him, not as my father but as a man in his own right. I recalled his bookshelves full of fierce sermons written by his father. I remembered the stories of how his mother, a Latin teacher, got her family through the Great Depression on a minister's salary. I imagined a dinner table with four children sitting before plates that held the legendary bacon ends, lemons and day-old bread. My dad was the youngest boy. In old pictures, he wore round thick glasses and suspenders on his shorts. Maybe he left the table hungry. Maybe in a time of want, the Holy Communion his father dictated seemed like food, a matter of survival. So he would dictate it to his children in turn because he wanted us to survive. When I viewed my father as simply wanting me to survive, my alienation seemed like a big misunderstanding. I wanted to acknowledge his love and let go of my resentment.

But with my son, I didn't get to choose. It was up to him.

Everything that mattered most felt beyond my control. Paradoxically, prayer seemed my only hope. From my liminal awareness, I sent my son the message that I would always do my best for him and I would always love him. That was a fundamental fact of my life. As I lay in bed that night, I wondered if my father had made the same prayer.

I dream I am cooking muffins in my friend Tzeporah's kitchen. My son comes up behind me and rests his arms around my shoulders. He is hugging me, no, holding me, from the back in a relaxed, casual way. It is as though the dream is taking place in a future time when all has been well for quite a while, and I have no reason to be surprised by this show of affection.

The sensation is pure numen—the accumulated joy of the countless hours I have held him, nursed him, read to him. It is condensed into ten seconds of all-encompassing touch. Gladness torches through my body. Then he moves on, and his friends come in. They talk and laugh around me as I cook.

Jung would call this a compensatory dream, my unconscious striving to balance my fear and separation with closeness and love. But that does not describe how this dream felt. It felt like true evidence that at some deep level my son and I had access to each other. Our love could still get through. That was all I wanted from the world.

Well, not quite all.

I wanted health for my family. That weekend, my husband sent the x-rays of our son's ankle to a friend in the States, who showed it to three radiologist colleagues. They each confirmed, independently, that the bony lump was osteochondroma, a benign growth. I found my son in his room with a friend. They lay on the bed, laughing at something on a computer screen. I pronounced that three doctors independently concurred that the tumour was benign as if I was commuting a death sentence. Me and my big emotions.

"Thanks, Mom," he said. "Now will you please get out of my room?"

Both Carl Jung and Jonathon Crary wrote about the role of dreams in the health of our larger culture. Basically, they both believe that myths and dreams can serve as social glue, presenting solutions to societal problems. I was drawn to this idea, although relying on dreams to guide society seemed suspect. Hadn't people always used visions to gain power by legitimizing their ideas into the word of god?

At a family reunion, I decided to test the disrepute of dreams by asking my relatives if they remembered theirs. The four-year-olds found the question exciting.

"I have Rapunzel dreams," my great-niece said and stroked her curls. "You know, her long, long hair."

"I dreamed I was Superman," my great-nephew said and spread his arms.

Everyone smiled at how cute this was and then resumed adult conversation, the day-world stuff.

But maybe we live in a time when we particularly need dreams, as we hover on the precipice of climate change. The only thing we can be sure of is that the world will be, is, fundamentally different than it has been over the 10,000 years in which modern society took shape. It will be fundamentally different than the world our species evolved in over the last 200,000 years.

Crary views dreams in the context of planetary destruction. He thinks they may be a way back to "a shared world whose fate is not terminal," an opportunity to rehearse the outlines of the deep renewal that our society desperately needs.

As far as I know, dreams haven't entered the climate change conversation in any form. The climate news is a relentless combination of terrifying data and the lack of political will to address it, with some small bright spots along the way. It is hard to imagine something as subjective as dreams playing a role. On the other hand, the data/politics approach isn't inspiring enough people to believe that climate change is their problem that they can solve. Maybe change needs deeper, more psychological roots. With all this rolling round in my head, I decided to test the premise that dreams could have a role. When I went to bed that night, I asked the dream maker for a dream about climate change.

In the first dream, I am crew on a large yellow rowboat. A few of us row and row, but always end up at the same shop to use the washroom and eat. My shirt wears out along the arm seams, and I need more sun protection, so I go belowdecks to look for my dry bag. The boat is much larger than I'd thought, with big closets, a kitchen and a hatch door to a huge carpeted room where a dozen more crew members lounge on bunk beds and play cards at a table.

"No wonder we aren't getting anywhere," I think. "The boat is too big, and only a few people are rowing."

If only the entire crew went on deck, they would realize how much they were needed, and they would want to row. After all, rowing is fun. It is what we are here to do. But before I can explain it, I awaken.

In the second dream, I sit on a bench in a snow structure built in the highest tree like a huge nest. I push lightly on the snow railing next to me, and it breaks off and falls to the ground below. I inch back toward the center of the structure, thinking it will hold, but it doesn't. The whole snow nest slowly breaks apart. As I fall through the air to the tree canopy below, I wonder if my injuries will be permanent and how they will affect my life.

Both dreams reflected my perspective on climate change: that we're all in the same boat, we need all hands on deck, and addressing it satisfies a deep drive toward species survival. Our place in the world is weakening more quickly than expected, and we don't know how we will land.

But my dreams lacked the broad cultural answer, the one that would compel a new way of being in the world, an affirmation that human compassion and creativity can carry our species through to survival. Night after night, I ask for the dream of renewal. So far it hasn't come.

Still, I am grateful that Numen Land gives me an occasional god-like nod of the head that is tailored to my very particular quandaries. I am grateful that every night my mind can relax into an immense, wildly creative sphere, and that in the day world, I feel increasingly rooted in its fertile field. I'm also glad that my ravenous sleep habits divert me from ravenous consumer habits like air travel and buying more shoes.

But I'll keep seeking a deeply shared dream that can animate us to uphold the life and beauty of the world. I'll search Numen Land for traces of the evolutionary wisdom left by our ancestors whose creativity helped them survive times of immense uncertainty. Maybe the shared dream will bubble up out of Numen Land's exuberantly generative force, the way it constantly creates new forms with nature's own persistence.

CHAPTER ELEVEN

River Creatures

W HEN HOLTON asked me if I wanted to go on a two-
week raft trip through the Grand Canyon, I was the
first person to pay the deposit. Friends had mythic stories
about the raft trips they went on every few years. One got bit-
ten by a scorpion. "I don't believe in animal medicine," she said,
"but for the next couple of years, that venom made me sting
when someone wasn't being completely honest." Another friend
told me about a day hike on which she cried and yelled. "People
thought I was going nuts," she said, "but I had just quit a job
and needed to get rid of the hard parts of it. Then I could see
what I had accomplished." They all described something along
the lines of becoming ancestral villagers as they traveled in a
small group through a wild place.

Six months later, 20 of us lined up in the dirt parking lot
of Lee's Ferry and passed blue rubber cylinders back and forth
from the bus to the rafts. My dry bag was crammed full of solutions for every possibility that might arise during a two-week
Grand Canyon river trip: field guides, a novel, art supplies and
a solar battery charger. I had even commandeered a second bag,
devoted wholly to the wet suit gear in which I hoped to swim
big portions of the river.

As I passed along each leaden bag, it occurred to me that perhaps river creatures pack based on how much they want to carry rather than on everything they could possibly need. Through the next two weeks, my bag became my karma, a weighty burden of purely aspirational tools that I carried across a dozen sandbars.

When we finished the dry bag bucket brigade, we sat down on life jackets and retreated from the glare beneath big hats and sunglasses to behold six river creatures. Three had broad shoulders, rounded bodies and easy smiles, as if the river had plumped them up with gregarious vitality. On a city street, one might notice in them the whiff of a bigger place. The other three were older, long and stringy, as if the river, over time, left only the essentials. I had trouble even picturing them on a sidewalk.

Lynn, the lanky trip leader, wore plaid pajama bottoms, a fish-patterned shirt and yellow camouflage gloves. He peered at us through thick round glasses and, with bashful resignation, began turning yet another group of clean, over-equipped strangers into river creatures.

First off, he told us to pee in the river. Otherwise, the campsites would stink of urine because the Grand Canyon gets such heavy use. If we didn't want to just squat at the river's edge, we could hide behind a bush and pee in the little plastic tubs that the company had provided. In camp, we would use a communal pee bucket.

"One woman put her entire weight on the big pee bucket in camp," he said. "It didn't hold. She fell onto the ground, and the pee poured over her."

He paused while we considered this woman's misfortune. Humiliated panic rose within me. Peeing in public is way too personal. Crouching by a river in full view was not going to happen. Where had I put that plastic tub?

Next, Lynn described a guest whose life jacket blew away in a wind storm. "That rafter had to hike up seven thousand feet in seven miles to get out of the canyon," Lynn said with gentle remonstration, "because a rafter who loses their life jacket becomes a hiker."

After the lecture, we got to choose our boats. Five were rowed by guides, and one was paddled by eight guests. I chose the paddle boat because I love physical work. I learned quickly that Rob, the blue-eyed, silver-haired paddle boat captain, could shout commands like a general or pose inviting questions like a psychologist. He had run the river almost two hundred times, first as the son of the owner of the AZRA Company, then as the owner and now as a guide emeritus in his daughter's company. He guides if and when he chooses, and he chose our group, dominated by returnees who were reputed to be environmental champions who lived large. Our group included the owners of an organic fair trade coffee company, two well-known climate activists and others who did their best to infuse their work with values. But our strongest link was geographical: our small island off the coast of British Columbia. Rob appreciated that as well.

I asked Rob how geography had shaped him as someone who had spent so much of his life in the Grand Canyon. Rob said the descent through hundreds of millions of years of rock became like a journey into deeper parts of his mind. The layers of sedimentary rock that form the canyon walls get older as you proceed down the river. Near the top, the wind-rippled sand dunes of the Colorado Plateau desert of 275 million years ago hardened into Coconino sandstone. Further along and deeper down, creatures that lived in a warm shallow sea 505 million years ago form the greyish Muav limestone. For Rob, descending the Colorado River means a journey into the immensity of geological time.

"As I raft further down the river, I go deeper into my unconscious mind," Rob said. "Eventually, I feel connected to all of life and all that life has been. Being down here can be a transformative experience, for those who are ready."

As I dug my paddle into the sleek, dimpled water, I wondered if I was ready to transform. I thought about my mom, how exactly a year ago she got sick. I remembered how tiny she looked, beneath a tangle of cardiac monitors, IV lines and an oxygen mask. I still felt fierce grief at losing her.

And then, of course, there was climate change. I'd spent five years writing about it for a news blog. Most recently, I reported on a two-day conference on natural gas attended by government leaders, oil company executives and Asian investors, in which they strategized how to fast-track development of liquefied fracked gas for export from British Columbia. I spent another two days writing an article that questioned this as a jobs strategy and pointed to studies that show natural gas might be equivalent to coal in CO_2 emissions. The article got 48 Facebook "likes," not very many by my standards. I felt like a kitten mewing at a tornado. I stopped writing.

I could always just have fun with all that water to immerse myself in. During the months prior to the raft trip, I developed an elaborate fantasy about swimming the Grand Canyon. I googled the idea and found a book that I devoured on the bus trip from Vancouver, BC, to Flagstaff, Arizona. In *We Swam the Grand Canyon*, Bill Beers described his 1955 trip with John Daggett. At that time, only 200 people had travelled the Grand Canyon by boat, and no one had swum it. Daggett had lost his family in an unnamed tragedy. Beers hoped the adventure would distract Daggett from sorrow, if it didn't kill them in the process. They put all their food and gear in rubberized boxes, donned rubber shirts and long johns and jumped in. When they got hypothermic, they torched beaches loaded with drift-wood. When their feet got raw from the constant submersion and rasp of the sand, they crawled around camp. When the National Park Service apprehended them because swimming the canyon was illegal, they argued that if they didn't capture this "first," other people would try. The Park Superintendent let them continue. When I read that their hands and feet were a mass of cuts and scrapes, that they were constantly cold and that they were having fun, my mind erased all the words but "fun." I also forgot the word "illegal."

"It's illegal, you know," Lynn told me when I broached the topic during our first night camped on the river. "Only training swims are allowed."

"I need some training," I said. "I'm not sure what would hap-pen were I to fall from a boat."

He told me about three women who ran the river in 2000 on riverboards, which are similar to beefed-up body-surfing boards. Then they travelled to rivers around the world on friendship missions.

"I want to do that too!" I exclaimed.

"Kelley Kalafatich got a parasite in Africa," he said. "Now she's paralyzed from the waist down."

I took in the tragedy of this but rejected it as a cautionary tale.

"There aren't parasites here."

"I suppose you can do a few training swims." Lynn looked pained. "But not yet."

The third night in, we squished our tents against a canyon wall at the top of a slope of pale orange sand. Dinner was punctu-ated by people running after their tents as the wind dragged them slowly down the slope to the river, even though we had placed big rocks inside as anchors. Blowing sand permeated every bag and sock. Ricardo, an entrepreneur who owns land near Cortes, tipped his wine glass to drink, and a trickle of sand landed in his lap.

"I think I have some sand in my sand," he said. I told him Beers, the swimmer, wore a swim mask in camp to keep the sand out of his eyes, and he asked for my swim goggles.

Later, I dozed between layers of the fine sand that had sifted in through the tent windows and listened to the tent fly thwap. My friend Annie was camped next to me. I met her on an organic farm on Cortes Island in 1994, a tomboy-type poet who teaches at a Native American college in Santa Fe. She visits me on Cortes Island most summers for kayaking and camping adventures. If she calls an adventure "bad," I feel especially complimented because she's so hard to tire out. In the canyon, we pitched our tents next to each other every night, or shared a tarp under the stars.

"Psst, Carrie." Annie stood outside my tent, urgent. "I can't find my life jacket. I think it blew away."

"Mmmm?" I asked.

"I don't want to hike out," she moaned.

I remembered seeing it plastered to a bush somewhere nearby.

"It's behind my tent," I said.

"Found it!" she called and returned through the dark to her tent to sleep, clutching her life jacket to her chest.

The next night was still. Annie and I laid our tarp and sleeping bags on a bluff above a broad part of the river where the swirls of an eddy the size of a baseball field shone under the light of a young moon.

"There's something about the juxtaposition of water flowing past rocks that are hundreds of millions years old that makes me feel like I have entered a different world," Annie said.

"The weird thing to me is that the Grand Canyon's top layers are from the Permian Extinction and the bottom layers from the Cambrian Explosion," I said. "Those are the only two geological events I can ever remember."

They weren't the only big events. The whole concept of geological periods is based on the five big extinctions that left empty niches for different life-forms to fill. I have difficulty keeping track of the ages in which fish, trilobites, birds and dinosaurs became most prominent. But it seems important to know about the Cambrian Explosion and Permian Extinction, the two biggest events that have occurred so far on Earth.

During the Cambrian Explosion, a mere 542 million years ago, life made a high-speed transition from blue-green algae—an oxygen-producing scum that had set the stage over four billion years—to a greater diversity of life-forms than at any other time on Earth. Bizarre creatures, including the ancestor of all vertebrates, swam in a giant sea surrounding the single lifeless continent. Some of those creatures became Grand Canyon limestone.

Three hundred million years later, Kapow! the Permian Extinction killed over 90 percent of all marine species. Vast swathes of ocean life died when carbon dioxide created anoxic dead zones. Calcium-based shells and plankton dissolved in the acidic water. No one knows what caused the massive emissions of carbon dioxide, but volcanic vents in what is now Russia seem most likely. The Permian Extinction sticks in my mind because some biologists think we may be at the beginning of an extinction event of similar magnitude.

What puzzled me was the unlikelihood that the Grand Canyon would capture this particular ten percent of Earth's history, between the creation of complex life and the biggest extinction yet. It's like a library caught fire and every book burned except the works of Shakespeare.

One of the guides, Bradford, knows as much as anyone in the world about the Grand Canyon. He's skinny and laconic, as habituated to the canyon as the rattler I saw looped between the stones of an old pueblo ruin. I asked him why the Grand Canyon rocks were sandwiched by these two events.

"I think about that a lot," he said. "It might have just happened that way. Something had to happen, and that is what did."

It seemed so improbable. But so did everything else that I really paid attention to.

The guides gave us lots of mind-bending geology to contemplate in the mornings after we stumbled to the makeshift kitchen for coffee. They drew pictures in the sand with sticks and did tricky dramatizations using cookie sheets to show how the Colorado Plateau was covered with shallow seas rich with life that receded and flooded again. Ribbons of land slammed into continents. Wind swept the sand into ridges that became stone. Rivers flopped around, in and out of their beds.

John McPhee wrote that, if humans could see on a geological time scale, "continents would crawl like amoebae, rivers would arrive and disappear like rainstreaks down an umbrella, lakes would go away like puddles after rain."

I started to see past the Grand Canyon's picture-postcard beauty as though I were looking through one of those old stereoscopes that give two-dimensional pictures a sudden depth of field. The brilliant orange cliffs deepened into a primordial story in which continents, ecosystems and life-forms rose and fell, merged and divided, restless and magnificent.

Each morning, we chose what boat to ride in: one of the two dories hand-built by Bradford, one of the three rafts rowed by guides or the paddle raft. Guests in the dories and rowing rafts lounged in the front and back except during rapids when they gripped the webbing straps to keep from getting thrown out of the boat. In the dories, they both gripped and bailed out the water splashed in by the rapids. I preferred the paddle raft for its camaraderie and the direct participation with the river, especially through the rapids.

Side channels flow into the Colorado River through gashes in the Grand Canyon's vertical cliffs. The rapids are formed by rare and inconceivable torrents that sweep through them leaving car-sized boulders in the main channel. Most of these rapids are bouncy and fun, but about 15 are big enough to flip boats and eject passengers. From the paddle raft, these rapids rumble unseen except for foam banners that snap above the lip where the water drops off. Before the drop, the river goes taut like shiny plastic food wrap.

At one of the larger rapids, Rob shouted "Stop!" and we floated, paddles across our laps, down the V-shaped tongue that glistened like a speeding ocean wave just before the peak curls.

From the tongue of water, the paddle raft descended nose first into a hole and rose toward a wall of foam where the water rejoined. We smashed through it.

"Hard forward!" Rob barked.

"Hard forward!" the four paddlers in the back of the boat echoed for the benefit of the front two paddlers, who are able to hear only the tumult of water and the crunching of raincoat hoods cinched against their ears.

We stretched out to plunge our paddles into rising mounds of water. Then we leaned back against the force. We rolled over

the top into the next hole brimmed by a white wall as tall as
the boat and burst through the spume. I got washed from the
left front toward the center of the boat. As the water receded,
I found the bottom and regained the stability of the paddle
stroke, the rhythmic order of biting into crest after crest. We
headed toward a wall where the current ricocheted left.

"Hard left!" Rob shouted. This meant—what did it mean?
My lifelong hesitation about lefts and rights had been exacer-
bated by switching sides, and I had to think through every di-
rectional command. I was on the left, so that meant to keep
paddling. I dug my paddle into the water for a few strokes and
then remembered—"left" meant I should back paddle. I plunged
the paddle behind me and leaned forward until the nose slowly
turned from the wall and the current pillowed us back into
the central channel of purling rollers. They dashed the raft and
soaked us and eventually subsided into a wave train of stroke
into *crest*, stroke into *crest*. Then the river shrugged into a sheet
of glossy swirls that plucked at paddle tips. Rob yelled, "Stop—
And—Rest," every syllable articulated with military precision.

We placed the paddles in our laps. At Rob's command,
we raised them up to touch in celebration of safe passage and
splashed them down on the river.

"Did you notice how long it took to turn from the wall?" he
asked. "That was weird."

"That was me," I muttered. "I got mixed up." He looked surprised, a flash of annoyance. I was in the paddle boat every day,
a protégé, eager to learn steering the raft. I should have known
better.

"Hard forward!" Rob called a moment later, but it was too
late, we were caught by conflicting currents that roiled and
yanked the boat toward an eddy's slow revolution back up the
river's edge. We stroked as hard as we could, but the current
pulled us upstream.

"Stop!"

The raft drifted 20 meters up the river until the eddy curled back toward the main current. Rob leaned on his paddle off the back of the boat and pivoted it to a 45-degree angle.

"Forward!" he shouted.

This time, we slipped easily through the "fence" between the main current and the eddy, and paddled toward the river's swiftest flow.

In the calm, we unclipped water bottles and day bags from their carabiners to apply sunscreen and rehydrate. Rob passed around a container of little pretzel squares full of peanut butter. At first I gave them a pass. The next time around, I tried one. The third time, I dumped them into my hand, the start of a two-week love affair with those trashy little salt bombs.

"Mosey," Rob called.

We jostled everything back into place and looked to the front-right paddler to set the cadence: stroke, stroke and rest the paddle on our laps for a second of complete relaxation; stroke, stroke, rest, gliding along the river's gentle push. Cracked orange monoliths rose to the narrow slice of sky above the canyon where thousands of swifts tucked and glided. Barrel cacti leaned toward us from streamside boulders, as if for a better view.

I've known Holton's daughter Sofia since she was two. Now a teenager, she made fun of me for hiding in the bushes with my pee bucket.

"That's ridiculous," she said one morning as I emerged from behind a bush. "I've seen you skinny-dip my whole life. You're one of the least modest people I've ever met."

"I know!" I wailed. "It *is* ridiculous. And my pee bucket has cracked."

I had no choice in the matter, so I peed at the river's edge with the expression of injured dignity that I learned from my cat. Sofia gave me knowing looks as I started my longish tramps along the river bank.

Holton didn't cut me slack either. As both an artist and clown, he likes to name unpleasant truths. One day at lunch, he hiked behind me up to ancient pueblo granaries high above the river.

"Lard ass," he hissed. "I know it bugs you."

"Thanks, Holton," I said.

His wicked bit of witness-bearing made me laugh. But still. I turned around and grabbed his chin and cheeks with one hand.

"I love you so much, Holton," I said, and affectionately squeezed his face until he looked like a fish.

In the dusk, Annie and I watched a sphinx moth the size of a hummingbird hover over an evening primrose and then trudged up the hill. We liked sleeping places with a wild tang and big sky, even if it meant several long trips hauling our blue cylinders, tents and sleeping kit.

We were working on ways to comprehend geological time. We hadn't noticed how, on the first few miles of the river, you can see the canyon's oldest sedimentary rock, 1.2 billion years old. Above that, about 900 million years of sediment had built up and then washed away, creating something known as an "un-conformity," in which rocks of hugely different ages rest on each other. The stupendous orange-red walls are only a few hundred million years old.

"Even a few hundred million years will take brain acrobat-ics," Annie said.

I told her about a time line we created for the kids at Linnaea

School. We tromped across three pastures unwinding colored twine that represented the geological ages. Two and a half fields were brown twine, representing the eons of blue-green algae. The kids had done projects on prehistorical creatures, and most of them were clustered at the yellow twine, the age of dinosaurs, a few inches from the end. Human life was overrepresented by a black pen mark right where the twine ran out.

"That's just sad," one of the kids said.

That was the crux of our problem: biographical time gets overwhelmed by geological time. But even biographical time seems overwhelming. A friend who had encountered a 12,000-year-old Clovis arrowhead laying in the bushes near a ruin in Utah had once described trying to imagine the lifetimes represented by the time span since that arrowhead was made, how the people in it had similar dreams and pain and happiness.

"Those people thought they were it," she said. "Then I think about how small humans are in the history of Earth as a whole, and so many neurons go off in my brain that my head might explode."

We were grateful for the creation myth that a young Navajo woman who works for the AZRA raft company told us one night around the campfire. It seemed calculated to relieve such neuronal pressures.

"The elders were putting stars in the sky, one by one, very intentionally and thoughtfully," she said. "Maybe even too thoughtfully. Coyote was extremely eager to help. But the elders wouldn't let him. They thought he'd make a mess of things. Coyote watched them work for a while, but they were so slow that he couldn't hold back any longer. He took the blanket where the elders had laid out the stars and flicked it, as hard as he could. All the stars flew up to the sky in a big higgledy-piggledy mess."

Annie and I thought that, if the stars can contain both intention and chaos, maybe personal meaning can exist in geological time. We especially liked how the story seemed to say, "Lighten up! Nice sky tonight!"

It *was* a nice sky, messy with constellations. And we had stayed awake long enough to see how they all revolve around the North Star.

Rob encouraged me to try captaining the paddle raft.

"Sixty percent of the job is reading the river," he said. "Forty percent is knowing how to steer."

He taught me to see the trail of bubbles that rises along the fastest water currents. I steered for this effervescent trail of swiftest flow. In the late afternoon, it became a river of light.

Every evening, I asked Lynn about my training swim. On the sixth day, he told me the rapid just below the camp had the right conditions. I ate breakfast in my wet suit and, as the boats launched, put my gear in Kelly's raft. Kelly has red hair, blue eyes and the most honest personality I've ever come across. She loves the river completely and understood my desire to be in it. She rows in a mini-skirt and knee-high neoprene boots, but I knew from her shoulders that she could pluck me from the water in an instant.

She pushed off, and I dove in. I stroked hard toward the opposite side of the river as chilly water seeped through the zipper at the back of my wet suit. Goggles gouged the bridge of my nose. When I reached the smooth fast tongue of water, the current sped me along, and I watched the waves curl down on either side before I dropped into a small hole. I bounced back up, and a river wave crashed in my face. Then I dropped into the next hole. There was a rhythm to it, down and up, bobbing like a cork. Kelly and I patted our heads across the white water, the signal that it's all fine.

"You look like an otter!" she yelled.

Friends in other boats cheered and called, "Is it hard?" They told me I was courageous, and strong for tolerating the cold.

In fact, it was pure fun. When the water lifted me upright into the feathery wave peaks, I kicked to go even higher. I rolled into waves and swam upstream to prolong the rush and tumble. As the wave train subsided, I felt the deep tug of the eddy fence at my feet and kicked away. In the calm, I lay on my back and watched the swifts flutter and barrel roll between the lofty red walls. The water's squeeze comforted me. The currents diverged in the river's depths and pulled my feet one way, my arms another. I kicked with my torso like a dolphin.

Nine shorebirds, avocets with tawny heads and long black legs, watched me from a sandbar as I rode the currents like a lumbering butterfly. Water spun me around. I felt like a tiny joyous squiggle in the canyon's book of time.

Some nights, to conserve the firewood we had to carry with us, we used a plastic bucket over a flashlight for a campfire. One night around the bucket, the Canadian climate activists described their work to the Americans. Gillian said she watched birds and sea life die in oil from the *Exxon Valdez* on TV when she was twelve and promised to do what she could to prevent future disasters.

"Canadians have always been proud of their role as global citizens," she said. "We were the first to speak out against apartheid, we were proactive in solving acid rain and we hosted the Montreal Protocol to protect the ozone layer. It's hard to imagine, but the country has fundamentally changed, to the extent that the Harper government is muzzling scientists to hide research that could hurt the oil industry."

Cara described growing up on the Canadian side of Niagara Falls near Love Canal, one of the most infamous toxic waste dumps. When she learned that the wild places she played in were toxic, she decided to work for doing things a better way.

"We need positive stories," she said. I'd noticed that "positive stories" are an important strategy for climate activists. According to the theory, the fact that climate change is fundamentally changing life on Earth in a way that will cause untold suffering is insufficient. Activists have to come up with more specific stories about why climate change matters.

In my mind's eye, I saw Winston Churchill shake his weighty head. Maybe it would remind him of the years in which his warnings about Hitler fell upon deaf ears. He believed in people's moral compulsion to eventually respond to a real and present danger. In his later writing, he laid the nation's survival during the time before the Americans joined the war at the unfaltering feet of the British citizens.

"It can't all be about what happens with a two-, four- or six-degree rise in temperature," Cara concluded.

"What *does* happen with a four-degree rise in temperature?" one of the New Yorkers asked.

"On our current path, four degrees will happen by 2050, and your island will be underwater," Cara said. This seemed to be news for most people in the group.

"My generation doesn't feel a lot of urgency about this," Sofia said, "but I'm seventeen, and when I hear that in 2050 my city will be underwater, that terrifies me."

To me, Sofia's family *is* New York, generations of world-famous artists, brilliant immigrants and canny developers.

She's a witty, creative, engaged young person. Her terror was my relief.

We talked about the cities and nations that would be submerged in the two-, four- and six-degree scenarios, as well as the droughts and famine, the floods and the mega-storms.

"It's just too depressing," someone said. The group fell quiet.

"Let's hold hands and picture what each of us sees as the solution," one of the guides suggested.

We took each other's hands. When I closed my eyes, it felt like what we imagined together had a place among the forces of the world. When we opened our eyes, a frog was leaping up the sides of the plastic bucket, attracted by the light.

Word got around that I had taken the bus from Vancouver to Arizona because I no longer fly. Ricardo, who has a private jet, had given several other guests a ride from Seattle. I felt linked to Ricardo because his wife had died a few months after my mom. I knew his was the more profound loss, and I made sure to say his wife's name out loud to him now and then because I longed to hear my mother's name on other people's lips. Ricardo appreciated it, and sometimes we talked at the wine bar. One night, he poured some wine he thought was particularly good into my stainless steel cup.

"What if there was one space on an airplane that was going to where you wanted?" he asked. "Occupying that empty seat wouldn't make any difference in carbon emissions."

I imagined getting to Seattle in two hours, surrounded by friends, instead of the three-and-a-half-day journey by Greyhound bus.

"I don't want to contribute to the demand," I said. "The emissions are so much higher than anything else I do. I'm just not comfortable with it."

We stared at our feet sunk into the peach-colored sand. I wanted him to know I was past the expectation that other people would feel similarly compelled.

"I know I'm just one person," I said. "That makes it sort of meaningless."

"I see the meaning," Ricardo said.

Some side canyons have layered walls with curves that undulate above the cool creek beds within. Others, like Lava Canyon at Mile 66, are broad sun-beaten valleys striped with eroding stone. Our group wandered up a tiny stream toward a distant cliff capped by a snail-shaped rock outcrop.

Annie and I stopped at a confluence of creeks beside stone layers of orange, green, purple and red. From the shade of a cottonwood tree, we viewed baked hills dotted with plants: dormant Acacia trees that looked like they had been torched; brittle bushes with yellow blooms and low purple blobs of milk vetch. Next to us, the thin creek splashed down a larger bed where a flash flood had left wads of grasses and sticks four feet high in the bushes.

"Does being in the Grand Canyon affect how you see climate change?" Annie asked.

"The layers of ancient rocks help me feel what a brief time I'm in," I said. "It's hard to see a way forward for humans from where we are now. What will our dust layer be? I wish I felt more hope."

"For me, hope is separate from the satisfaction of being engaged," Annie said. "I hold on to the place of 'don't know.' There's ethical meaning in reckoning with climate change, even if I don't feel necessarily hopeful. It's just a more satisfying way to live."

Our friend Christian, a German geologist, would shake his head at my longing for hope and Annie's search for ethical meaning. He thinks we're doomed and hope is irrational, but it doesn't bother him.

"Christian thinks that, no matter how this ride will end up, it is absolutely sensational to have been given a ticket at all," I said. "But I wonder about that. We're just starting the most intense period of change humans have ever faced, and I want to know there will be a humane, civilized transition. If we don't leap through that closing window, I want to know that the world built on the ashes of this one will include the joy of being human."

"We can't know," Annie said. She described a meditation retreat she had attended in New Mexico that used as a koan "irreconcilable loss." During the retreat, huge forest fires burned in the mountains across the valley. Every day they awoke to smoke and flames. Climate change was right there, destroying the forests they loved.

"We were breathing the loss of climate change," Annie said. "It was so much bigger than we could honor or grieve. There's such irreconcilable loss."

"And unrequited love," I said. "I love the Earth so much as it is now, and I want to hold on to it but I can't."

We left the creek and wandered up a stony ridge to a plateau where plants grew around a central rock. Banana yuccas' waxy blossoms drooped from central spikes with surprising luxuriance for such a dry place. Purple-flowered prickly pears circled the yucca, and yellow-flowered brittle bush grew further out from the boulder in a wavy ring. It seemed designed by relationships, a mesh of invisible agreements that gave each plant a place to thrive.

Rapids are rated on a scale from one to ten, and Crystal Rapids, close to Mile 100, was our first ten. Annie and I set up our tents high on a ridge overlooking the rapids. We found Lynn sitting on a stone looking down, so we cornered him for a conversation. We loved his combination of vulnerability and determination, and his odd style of rowing, first one oar then the other, shambling along the river, always in the lead.

Lynn preferred to look at the river as he spoke, except for quick glances when a deep twinkle would suddenly emerge from behind his glasses. Annie called this his existential "Hey!"

He told us Crystal Rapids were fairly new, the result of a 1966 debris flow from the Crystal River. The river had shifted the rocks downstream since then, some of them into a big boulder bar. We stared at the barrier across the river. The water whipped past on either side of it.

"You don't want to get stuck on that," he said.

He described how a baloney boat, one of the giant motorized rafts that take tourists on a faster trip through the canyon, got stuck there and then capsized.

"You don't seem too worried," Annie said.

"It's not that bad," he said. We knew he had been one of the world's best kayakers in the 1970s. The Grand Canyon, so imposing to us, was his retirement gig.

Choosing a path through the rapids depends on the water level. Our wild, pristine river rose and dropped every day at the behest of engineers at the Glen Canyon Dam upstream, built after environmentalists like Ed Abbey lost one of their most epic battles. We asked Lynn how long he thought the dam will survive.

"It almost blew in 1983," he said. "The whole thing was vibrating. But the water doesn't get that high anymore because of all the droughts. I think the river will just slowly work its way through the surrounding sedimentary rock, the same way it did with the lava dams further down the river. It will take a while."

"You can feel the spirits of the river guides here," he offered. "We've all left some part of our selves here at different times. You can feel them mulling around, looking down at Crystal."

Each of the other guides had wandered by, staring down into rapids where boat-high waves swarmed and churned. We asked Lynn how the guides chart their paths through the chaos.

"You can't control things once you're in," Lynn said. "You just study the rapids beforehand, choose your line and hope for the best."

After 13 days, the Grand Canyon's narrow walls had opened up into multi-tiered buttes. On the second-to-last day, the anniversary of my mother's death, we camped at Mile 199. I woke up crying. Annie wrote "Elie," my mom's name, in driftwood at the water's edge. I ate breakfast in my wet suit and put my gear in Bradford's dory because he was kind yet unlikely to make conversational demands. I asked him about the first rapid, one generally used for training swims.

"How would you recommend swimming this rapid?" I asked.

"I would never recommend swimming it at all," he said.

I rephrased my question.

"What line should I take going down the rapid?"

"Follow my boat," he said. "I'm heading to the left to get around the hole at the top."

The river jostled me through the rapids and gave me a hard race away from a wall. It held me through the calm waters. I curled up like a fetus and spread my limbs like a corpse. Its pressure displaced sorrow for the ebb of life with joy for the life of the river, for the rare privilege of being alive and free in such a stupendous place, of being alive and free at all.

I climbed on a sandbar and made a sand angel as ephemeral as my mom, as myself, as the Earth's gifts at that instant. Each moment glowed with improbability, anchored by the past that towered in the canyon walls. The creatures whose bodies became limestone, the river guides who searched for a path through the rapids, my mother, all of them had held the crux of existence before me. None of them got to preserve for all time what they loved, or even completely determine their own course. Like me, they had the opportunity to study the rapids, choose their path and find joy in the river's firm embrace.

CHAPTER TWELVE

The Scallop
and the Chickadee

"I CAN BARELY stand it," I confessed over G&Ts in my friend Chris's kitchen. He's a climate consultant who does things like write op-eds behind the scenes and take reporters on flights over the tar sands. Like me, he lacks a reflexively cheery outlook.

"How do you cope?" I asked, meaning climate change, knowing he would understand.

His green-flecked eyes locked on mine, and he stopped drying a wine glass. Around us, friends laughed loudly about cheerier topics.

"Mindfulness," he said. "And meditation."

Someone interrupted our conversation, so we left it at that.

Meditation wasn't in my blood. According to my religious conservative father, navel-gazing explained the poor physical conditions of entire nations while North America's postwar prosperity was due to the Protestant work ethic. His favorite saying demanded action: "If you're not part of the solution, you're part of the problem." I felt his bone-deep sense of public duty in my response to climate change, but none of his dynamic Christian faith to carry me through when the facts got overwhelming. And all of his kids were sticklers for facts. During dinner table debates, when my dad set down his fork to go in search of information, the five of us yelled after him, "Never mind, Dad. We don't care that much" and rolled our eyes in boredom while he read paragraph after paragraph from the *Encyclopedia Britannica*. But now we all emulate his pursuit of information, from in-the-moment fact-checking to evenings curled up with books like Bill Bryson's *A Short History of Nearly Everything*, E. O. Wilson's *The Future of Life* or James Hansen's *Storms of My Grandchildren*.

When I researched mindfulness meditation, I realized that I could have come to a dinner table debate armed with awesome evidence: regular meditation builds denser grey matter in the prefrontal cortices where more considered decisions are made and shrinks the regions of the brain associated with stress and reactivity. This less reactive response helps with all kinds of health problems: depression, addiction, smoking, overeating, ADHD, asthma and so on. Even hospitals use navel-gazing to reap its well documented results.

It was enough to spur me on. With less reactivity, I'd be able to stay abreast of the climate news without panicking. It might even reduce my extreme startle response, the loud gasp and spooky little dance in which I shake my arms and hop from leg to leg. Apparently, it's both unsettling and hugely annoying. So I signed up for an eight-week mindfulness class.

The first class was on ways of seeing. The teacher showed us a picture that could be viewed two different ways, as a young woman in a flowing headdress or an old woman in a cowl. Everyone could see the old woman but me. The class waited while another student pointed her out, feature by feature. Suddenly there she was, with a great big nose.

"Aaaaaah."

The class gave a collective sigh of relief. Afterward, I stopped at the adjacent florist shop and bought a beautiful pink rose, ostensibly as a valentine for my husband but also to celebrate finally seeing that old woman.

It was a remarkable rose, still pink and tender when class time rolled around again, well worthy of raving about to the florists, even though I was already a few minutes late. By the time I entered the adjacent classroom, everyone had laid out their yoga mats for a guided body scan.

"My mat!" I exclaimed, and rushed back out to my bike to get it.

On my second entry, the floor was covered with two rows of people lying on yoga mats. I wanted to join them, but I really had to pee. By my third entry, the teacher was telling everyone to be aware of the sensations in their toes: warmth, moisture, tingling or perhaps itching. I tiptoed through the feet that lay across the center of the room, laid out my mat and began to notice my toes. Then a cell phone went off at the far end of the room, a series of blasts on a goat horn. My cell phone. I started in recognition and glanced at the teacher. She gave me a crisp nod, so I tiptoed back through the feet, put my phone on vibrate and tiptoed through the feet one more time back to my mat. I lay down and, according to instruction, noted the sensations of my shins. Then suddenly the lights went on, and I awoke with a start.

As we put the chairs into a circle, I felt mortified for being so unmindful, even rude. To demonstrate my appreciation for the class, I filled every awkward pause during the following discussion with friendly commentary. Eventually, the teacher suggested that it was time to hear from other people.

People described their body scan experiences. Some couldn't feel their toes. Others itched all over. Then the teacher talked about how body awareness and mindfulness can increase the pleasure of everyday moments, such as eating good food and walking places. As a nurse, I'd learned to multitask, never walking those long corridors with less than three purposes in mind, and the habit gave my questions a common theme.

"Can you eat while you read and still be mindful? Or mindfully talk on the phone while you do dishes?"

"Just observe these things as you do them," she said. "Try not to judge them."

In the following days, this advice satisfied my love of multitasking by giving me a third thing to do, observing. There was even a fourth if you include "not judging" as its own thing, which in my experience it is. Single-minded mindfulness came only with intensely pleasurable activities, like eating gnocchi and scrubbing my back with a scratchy brush in the shower.

Our homework was to list a pleasant experience each day. I noted a new coffee drink with bitter chocolate and orange peel, riding my bike while looking at trees and how the kitty placed her paw on my hand to keep me near. But I resisted being mindful about certain pleasures, like eating chocolate. Mindfulness might threaten my ability to eat until I had a stomach ache, which gives me emotional satisfaction. The third week of class, I asked the teacher about mindfulness in things that you want to do but know you shouldn't, like eating too much chocolate.

"Just slow it down a little," she said. "Notice how it feels to put off the next bite. You might find you want less."

Exactly my point.

She talked about how pain is inevitable, but we overlay it with a lot of unnecessary suffering from resistance, anticipation, regret and implied meanings. She called too much of this kind of thinking "catastrophizing." I thought about how my son leaves his dishes in the sink instead of putting them in the dishwasher. "It's so disrespectful," I thought each time. "He knows how much I like a clean kitchen. I cook bacon just for him, why can't he just put his dish in the dishwasher for me? Maybe he'll expect his partner to clean up after him," and so on. But what if the dish was just a dish? What if he was a typical preoccupied teen who didn't have the bandwidth to consider how it felt to his mother? It was hard to get my mind around, but even considering the possibility opened things up a bit.

That week for homework, we wrote down unpleasant things and how we felt about them when we took a step back from our usual thoughts. I started small: riding my bike uphill in the rain, that same old hill below our house that I've dreaded a thousand times. And it wasn't that bad. In fact, once I decided not to dread it, I enjoyed it. Another transformation came with shaving my legs. I realized there was no point to my deep resentment. It's something I had decided to do for my city years, and at least one feminist friend claimed to find enjoyment in the task. My soapy skin was silky, and for once I didn't end up with a little anklet of hair.

I still had problems with the body scan that we were supposed to do every day. It was so soothing that it put me to sleep. In fact, I used it to fall asleep at night.

"Do you always fall asleep at the same point?" the instructor asked the next week.

I thought about it. I had scanned my feet, ankles, shins, knees and thighs a dozen times, but I had never scanned my pelvis.

"Yes," I answered.

"Where?"

"My pelvis."

"Hmm," she said. "That's interesting."

"Why?"

"It just is."

"To be honest, I find the body scan really boring," I said.

"Hmm," she said. "That's interesting. Is boredom bad?"

"Yes."

"It's not that big of a deal," she said. "It's not like physical pain."

This got me thinking. If boredom wasn't bad, I'd be a much different person. My dislike of boredom made me do things like issue precise commands to other mothers and kids at Lego Land so our little fire truck would win the race to the fake fire, rather than letting the kids bumble around and slowly figure it out for themselves. When a task was assigned at a meeting, I could have sat on my hands and breathed through the silence until some other person volunteered, instead of leaving with a huge task list and ultimately burning myself out. If I didn't dislike boredom, my husband wouldn't get annoyed with how fast I walk, bike, snorkel and so on. I'd have the patience to change my own bike tire and find my own keys. And really, boredom is not as bad as being poked by needles or going hungry day after day, even though it wouldn't build a nation like the Protestant work ethic did.

Next the teacher talked about responding rather than reacting. We were getting to the nub of my problem. When I look at climate news headlines, I react. First my chest tightens up, then my throat, and then my mouse heads for the website with pretty pictures from around the world to end the discomfort. Was it really possible to observe my reaction without trying to avoid it?

That week, Climate Progress reported on how ocean acidification killed ten million scallops off the coast of Vancouver Island. The familiar panic arose, but I stayed with the program. "Discomfort, how interesting." Deep breath, keep reading. I learned that the declining pH level off Vancouver Island dissolves the calcium in the shells of baby scallops and oysters, and the level of carbon dioxide in local waters was double its former normal range. I didn't catastrophize by imagining entirely dead acidic oceans and starving people. Maybe that won't happen. Maybe we'll act soon, suddenly even, once we reach a critical mass of awareness. The story made me sad, but not sick.

Later, as I rode my bike, I noted the pleasure of chickadees singing their "come hither" song on every block. "There's ocean acidification, and then there's chickadees," I thought. "There's sad, and then there's beautiful." The chickadees pulled me out of obsessing over the scallops, and this was useful.

The class moved on to actual meditation. My expectations were low, given my body scan failure (or, less judgmentally, nap issues) and my inherited prejudices against navel gazing. I once asked a meditating friend if she really didn't have anything better to do than stare at the floor in front of her.

But given the necessity of a new approach and promising research, I went after it hard. Every morning for 30 minutes, I focused on my breath, noted my thoughts, returned to my breath. I remembered metaphors for the mind, the crazed elephant, the wild stallion. It took a huge effort to rein in this unbiddable beast. If I managed to hold the stallion for a second or two, fiery itches erupted across my entire body. There was drama to it, oh yes, there was drama. Then I'd remember my breath again.

In the next class, the teacher talked about diet, the things we choose to take into our minds as well as our bodies. This reminded me of our friends Christian and Aileen who lived for 35 years on land that was off the grid with only boat access. I sent them a short essay I'd written with some of their stories from that time. Christian responded to my concern that "not enough happened" in the essay.

"Nothing happening" is the whole point of living the way we chose to live, to NOT overexcite the nervous system habitually. We don't want to be caught in the treadmill of seeking ever-escalating thrills. We want to be in a place where a baby muskrat tripping and falling off our deck into the pond is as dramatic as an L.A. drive-by shooting.

I realized they were decades ahead on the mindfulness diet.

The next weekend, I went surfing in Tofino on the west coast of Vancouver Island. I don't catch waves as they break because it feels safer to ride in on the post-break froth. If I fall off the board, I stay under for a while. But somehow my surfboard slammed into my face anyway, hard enough to make my teeth ache, for half my face to go numb and for blood to ooze out of my mouth. The next day, my swollen purple face made me look like an orc from the *Lord of the Rings* movies. At the coffee shop, fellow customers gave one shocked glance and looked away.

The experience provided two mindfulness nuggets. First, it was an overdue crash course in itchiness for someone who likes to scratch a mosquito bite until it bleeds. My upper lip stayed numb and yet itched like heck. When I scratched it, I couldn't feel any sensation. I witnessed my pointlessly firing neurons with no temptation of relief, while repeating to myself that no one ever died of an itch.

Second, because I looked like a battered woman, I holed up in bed with an ice pack and read many interesting things on Facebook. One story gave me an epiphany.

A monk was tired of his apprentice's complaints, so he told the apprentice to put a handful of salt in a glass of water and drink it. It was bitter, and the apprentice spat it out. Then the monk told the apprentice to put the same amount of salt in a lake and take a drink from that. The apprentice did so and reported that the lake water still tasted sweet. The monk explained that salt is like the pain of life: its taste depends on the size of the container you put it in. You can't avoid pain, he said, but you can make your container bigger.

Eureka! I thought. A bigger container was the common theme to my most precious adventures and experiences! In the Grand Canyon, geological time gave humans a place in the restless, magnificent story of continents and ecosystems. Numen Land provided a place of collective wisdom. First Nations cultures linked generations through place. Fulfilling my evolutionary legacy by being present at my mother's death joined me to the rest of humanity. My entanglement with pikas acknowledged an unseen interdependent web. Arne Naess's larger Self unified me with the natural world. Even trying to expand my community on a small island or swimming in the cold vast ocean created a container large enough to hold my woes and still retain the sweetness of being alive.

But in daily life, without those heightened physical experiences that plant me in the middle of everything, there's no big sweet lake. Maybe Chris found that mindfulness and meditation helped him cope with climate change because it brought the big lake into more mundane moments of existence, which is most of them. Sometimes during meditation, between the epic struggles with the crazed elephant and the slow march of the itch, existence simply commended itself. Likewise, mindfulness commended the sensations of being alive, like hearing the chickadees' song and feeling the kitty's paw.

At the very height of my epiphany, my inner dad interrupted with a comment that it looked a lot like navel-gazing to him. This took me aback. I got a fresh ice pack for my black eyes and had yet another long nap, which seems to be the only cure for a minor head injury.

When I awoke, a few political implications of mindfulness seemed easy enough. The first one was a corollary to the

chocolate question. In spite of myself, the more I paid attention to the chocolate I ate, the less I wanted and I didn't even
miss out on any of the emotional satisfaction. If I applied
mindfulness to my consumer habits, I'd want things that were
more aligned with my knowledge. I already eschewed palm oil
(deforestation, pygmy elephants) and octopus (damn, they're
smart). No hair shirt involved; awareness snuffed the desire.

Also, mindfulness lines up with Arne Naess's and Jonathon
Crary's suggestions that satisfaction arises separately from the
consumption of goods. Arne Naess's elegant idea that complexity of experience is achieved through simplicity of means
has mindfulness written all over it: the chickadee, the paw.
Jonathon Crary might equate meditation with sleep: less time
spent on fulfilling our function as consumers in a devastating
economy and more time spent in a mental state conducive to
developing shared goals.

And sorry, Dad, but the practices just don't invite escape.
They invite separating one's identity from one's thoughts so one
can see the world with great acuity. According to my mindfulness workbook, "*Your thoughts are not 'you' or 'reality.'*" The
Dalai Lama puts critical investigation at the heart of his tra-
dition. It shares the goal of science: understanding objective
reality.

That's as far as I could get before sleep dragged me under
yet again.

I woke up in time for our favorite late-night comedy show,
The Colbert Report. That night's guest was Dan Harris, a news
anchor on tour for his new book, *10% Happier*, a memoir about
his skeptical, amusing path from panic attacks in front of a
national news audience to a meditation practice. Avid for all
things meditation, I immediately downloaded the book and
read it between naps.

It turned out that Harris also worried that navel-gazing

might make a person happier at the price of being effective in the world. The concept of "nonattachment" helped him get past this. It meant striving for one's goals without the expectation of a certain outcome.

I'd had at least one amazing result with nonattachment. A dark and rainy night several years ago, industrial logging equipment hovered around the forest I had spent decades trying to protect. There was nothing left to do except create a "swan song," a *cri de coeur* to record my community's love and loss. A group of us wrote and posted an online petition that we sent to everyone we knew who loved the island. Seven thousand signatures later, we had lots of media attention, and the timber company asked us back to the negotiating room. It helped me see the value of political action simply as a form of creative expression. And, in fact, you just don't know what might come of it.

But Dan Harris wasn't making the point that if you don't expect it, it will come. His point was resilience:

> When you are wisely ambitious, you do everything you can to succeed but you are not attached to the outcome—so that if you fail, you will be maximally resilient, able to get up, dust yourself off, and get back into the fray.

Oddly enough, my father would have embraced this. His second favorite saying was, "The secret to success is to keep showing up."

By the end of the week, my mash-up of naps, climate change, mindfulness and meditation had incubated into some working hypotheses.

First, nonattachment is more useful to me than hope. Right now, not enough people know to demand a smooth transition to new energy systems, and oil companies are using their huge financial resources to keep things this way. So hope feels more like wishful thinking than a realistic assessment. Nonattachment, on the other hand, doesn't invite misjudgment or downfall.

Second, I desperately need resilience, and what do you know, it can be intentionally strengthened like a muscle. Meditation builds calm and creativity, while mindfulness builds appreciation for the sensations of being alive. To cope with climate change, I need this combination of determination, inspiration and *joie de vivre*.

Finally, our society gives me a lot of tools. There's the freedom of expression to campaign for climate candidates and to show up at climate stability rallies. I can write letters to government demanding a carbon tax to make oil companies pay for the destruction their product imposes on others and to create an even playing field for renewable energy sources. There's plenty of opportunity to express my sense of public duty and my *cri de coeur*. At a time when mass extinction is not at all farfetched, such rights feel extremely precious.

Over the course of the week, my bruised face improved, along with my mental outlook. The purple traveled from my eyes down into my cheeks and began to turn a greenish yellow. With dark glasses on, I looked mysterious and dramatic, perhaps a secret agent with a tropical disease. It would do. I felt ready to dive back in.

Climate Change 101:
The Basics

Here's some basic information on which to base a demand for political action on climate change. First, we can curb climate change and live safe, comfortable lives using existing technology. Second, the cost to employ existing technology is incredibly low compared to the cost of the coming climate damage. Third, every year of delay dramatically increases the eventual costs of climate damages, and not just in money. Inaction is a choice that results in widespread suffering.

Solution: Pay for pollution damage up front.

Experts call climate change the greatest market failure of all time because people causing the damage aren't paying for it. Other people are. The people who bear the brunt of changes in the weather systems aren't the big polluters. Climate costs include increasingly savage storms, droughts, famines and loss of land due to sea level rise. Younger and future generations face a much harsher world, but damage to North America is well underway: superstorms Sandy and Katrina, the drought in the southwest, massive forest die-off from the pine beetles, freshwater shortages and far larger wildfires, to name a few.*

What if we paid for the costs of likely damages from fossil fuels as part of the product price?

Competition would be on a more equal footing because we wouldn't all be subsidizing the fossil fuel companies by letting

* climate.nasa.gov/effects/

them destabilize the world without paying for it. We'd make different consumer choices. Renewable energy sources such as wind, solar and geothermal would become more competitive and grow faster. Innovation would have greater financial reward. A lot of economists think employment rates would increase because renewable energy creates more long-term jobs than capital-intensive fossil fuel industries. Economies could actually improve, but even if they didn't, we could avoid the immense disasters that climate change portends.

A price on climate pollution can take the form of a tax, regulation or a cap on emissions with a market for trading permits to pollute. A carbon tax seems simplest and has worked well in BC where emissions have dropped while the economy has grown relative to the rest of Canada. BC uses the carbon tax revenues to cut taxes elsewhere, so there is no net tax increase. Other studies confirm: a carbon tax decreases greenhouse gases, increases employment numbers and increases GDP in the economy as a whole.*

President Obama uses regulation to control climate pollution because Congress won't pass the necessary legislation. He made rules for new power plants and hopes to regulate how much existing plants can emit. It's a piecemeal approach that doesn't have as much incentive for innovation across all the economy's sectors.

The US successfully used cap and trade to solve the problem of acid rain. The European Union uses cap and trade for carbon and hopes its system will eventually be linked to other systems worldwide. The biggest advantage is that the emissions cap can be based on science and has more certain results than a carbon tax. Some critics say the European Union overallocated permits to pollute so the permits are too cheap, but

* grist.org/climate-energy/the-positive-economic-impact-of-a-carbon-tax -in-uh-hang-on-10-charts/

the amount will be ratcheted down over time. The system is market-driven and has helped set a price on carbon in jurisdictions that use it.

Whichever methods we choose, doing something is better than nothing because the costs of inaction vastly exceed the costs of action.*

Problem: Scary numbers.

350 ppm (parts per million) means there are 350 molecules of carbon for every million molecules in the air. This number is used by climate scientists to indicate the *safe level* of carbon dioxide in the atmosphere. There were 280 ppm prior to the Industrial Revolution, but 350 ppm may be still low enough to avoid triggering events which will accelerate climate changes beyond our control.

450 ppm means 450 molecules of carbon for every million molecules in the air. This is the number that virtually all climate scientists agree is the fall-off-the-cliff limit. At 450, it is clear there will be *unacceptable and irreversible damage.* 450 ppm is associated with a 2-degree Celsius temperature rise, which signatories to the Copenhagen Accord agreed would be the maximum acceptable amount of global temperature rise.

We are now at 400 ppm and rising, fast. For current levels, go to: esrl.noaa.gov/gmd/ccgg/trends/#mlo.

These numbers only allude to the complexity of the whole story. One way to think about rising carbon counts is that it loads the dice for certain rolls, and they are dangerous ones. The "bad things" might not happen, but they are far more likely to than if the dice weren't loaded. Higher numbers can now be rolled than the human species has ever experienced. The more parts per million of carbon dioxide, methane and other greenhouse gases in the atmosphere, the more likely we are to have megastorms, droughts, floods, wildfires, permafrost melt, loss

---

* un.org/climatechange/mitigation/economics/

of glaciers, change in ocean currents, crop losses, heat waves, increases in sea level, collapsed coral reefs, ocean acidification and the massive extinction of sea life that goes with it.

Many of these things are already happening and faster than scientists predicted. And the changes aren't always linear. It's like pushing a round stone towards a decline: once it starts to roll down, it will be out of our control. The result would be runaway climate change, and it would make life very hard, or even impossible, for human kind. This will happen if permafrost melts and releases enormous amounts of methane into the atmosphere, or if the oceans warm enough to melt the icy methane at the bottom of the ocean so it bubbles to the top, or if the forests die off in the Amazon and Boreal forests. If these massive storage areas for greenhouse gases are opened up, we won't be able to stop their release.

A World War II level of mobilization would be commensurate to the threat. But fossil fuel companies fund political campaigns at all levels of government and spread doubt about the science. Climate change solutions challenge many people's ideals of small government and national sovereignty because stabilizing the climate will require reining in some of the world's largest corporations and unprecedented international cooperation. Yet every one of us in every political party needs governments to act on quickly decreasing greenhouse gas emissions to secure our safety and that of young people who we love.

Right now we rely on oil, but having a climate stable world doesn't require us to live like we did in preindustrial times. Rather, it requires putting the true price on climate pollution to stimulate better design and use of the available clean technologies. Prevention costs much less money than dealing with climate damage, suffering has no price, and we're in this predicament with a lot of other creatures that don't want to go extinct either, like the pikas, the scallops and the chickadees.

Climate Change 201—Carrie's Suggestions
Favorite Books

Elizabeth Kolbert, *Field Notes of a Catastrophe* and *The Sixth Extinction*. Kolbert travels with scientists and tells their stories in a highly engaging manner. It's the crème brûlée of climate writing.

George Marshall, *Don't Even Think About It: Why Our Brains Are Wired to Ignore Climate Change*. Marshall compiles the most recent research on the slow uptake on climate action and how to foster deeper engagement.

George Monbiot, *Heat*. Explores what a climate safe society might look like.

Bill McKibben, *Eaarth*. Describes the changes already upon us and the need to change course while we can.

James B. MacKinnon, *The Once and Future World*. Looks at humans and nature in ways that are both beautiful and hopeful in the long view.

Favorite Websites

The preeminent climate blog is *Climate Progress*: thinkprogress .org/climate/issue/

The most entertaining blog with good climate coverage is *Grist*: grist.org

My husband Barry's writing and my writing, along with other excellent climate coverage, are at the *Vancouver Observer*: vancouverobserver.com

Barry's charts, which turn complex data into eye candy, can be viewed on our *Visual Carbon* website at saxifrages.org/eco/

Climate Change 301—Barry's Suggestions
Favorite Books

James Hansen, *Storms of My Grandchildren*. Climate Science 101 combined with behind-the-scenes tales of US climate politics by one of the world's foremost climate scientists.

J. Veron, *A Reef in Time: The Great Barrier Reef from Beginning to End.* One of the world's top coral reef experts explains how climate changes are already destroying the world's coral reefs and threatening them with global extinction.

Favorite Websites

Dr. Jeff Masters WunderBlog at wunderground.com/blog/Jeff Masters/show.html. A top meteorologist's explanation of the latest extreme weather events, often with an explanation of the role climate change might be playing in it.

The Daily Climate at dailyclimate.org/archives_tdc.jsp. A daily list of climate change articles pulled from the world's major media.

Skeptical Science at skepticalscience.com. Lists over 100 of the most common climate change myths and what the climate science says about them. Information helpfully organized into simple and more advanced explanations with great links to learn more.

US Government. An unbelievable amount of high quality information and detailed data on just above every aspect of climate change:

NOAA data at climate.gov

EPA climate portal at epa.gov/climatechange/

NASA data at climate.nasa.gov

EIA energy and CO_2 data at eia.gov/environment/

International Energy Agency at iea.org. Top source for global energy and climate pollution stats and trends. I often refer to their ETP scenarios for how the world can avoid dire climate changes through changes to our energy systems at iea.org/etp/explore/

Book Group Discussion Guide for *The Big Swim*

Science and spirituality

Describe the protagonist's relationship with nature. What is your relationship with nature? Example?

In "Deep Blueberry Gestalt," the protagonist expresses ambivalence about the idea of angels. How does this reflect how she relates science to spirituality? How does science influence your spirituality?

In "The Scallop and the Chickadee," the protagonist explores meditation and mindfulness as ways to manage the emotionally overwhelming aspects of climate change. What are those overwhelming aspects for her? What emotions come up for you in the face of climate change? How do you relate to them? What would help you?

How would you describe the protagonist's morality? Do you think her decision to not fly has added to or diminished her life satisfaction? In "River Creatures," Ricardo thinks her decision has meaning regardless of its impact. What do you think? Have you changed any behavior because of your understanding of climate change or another global issue? Explain what you did and how you came to the decision and what meaning this action has for you.

Culture

In "The Oolichan and the Snake," how do the First Nations elders convey their ethical perspectives and values? How are these perspectives different from the dominant cultural perspectives? Which do you think are more practical?

How does climate change raise different issues for people of different cultures and classes?

"Journey to Numen Land" presents Jonathon Crary's idea that society undervalues sleep and this has political implications. What do you think of this theory? Do you value sleep? Why or why not?

Philosophy

In "Deep Blueberry Gestalt," the protagonist considers Arne Naess's idea that the less one needs, the closer one comes to satisfying the ultimate goals of life. How might your life experiences substantiate this idea?

In "Nectar," the protagonist articulates the idea that she finds the greatest satisfaction in living the experiences that evolution prepared her for, such as being present for the death of a parent. Can you think of examples in this your life?

In "River Creatures," the protagonist contemplates how the vastness of geological time affects her sense of personal meaning. How does she reconcile geographical time with biographical time? How do you? How does geological time influence your view of climate change?

About the Author

CARRIE SAXIFRAGE is a journalist and author whose work on First Nations responses to the proposed Northern Gateway Pipeline has garnered significant critical acclaim. Her research and analytic skills were honed as an environmental lawyer in the US. Now she writes for the *Vancouver Observer* and homesteads on a remote BC island. Carrie's pursuit of adventure and love of nature has taken her up mountains like the Matterhorn and Chimborazo. In 2006 she committed herself to the most life-affirming adventure yet: a low carbon lifestyle.

Credit: Kris Krug staticphotography.com

The personal reward for climate action is an intensified sense of belonging and the satisfaction of contributing to a shared project. Climate change can bring us together. This is the real reward of taking action.

If you have enjoyed *The Big Swim*, you might also enjoy other

BOOKS TO BUILD A NEW SOCIETY

Our books provide positive solutions for people who
want to make a difference. We specialize in:

**Food & Gardening ◆ Resilience ◆ Sustainable Building
Climate Change ◆ Energy ◆ Health & Wellness
Sustainable Living ◆ Environment & Economy
Progressive Leadership ◆ Community
Educational & Parenting Resources**

New Society Publishers
ENVIRONMENTAL BENEFITS STATEMENT

New Society Publishers has chosen to produce this book on recycled paper made
with 100% post consumer waste, processed chlorine free, and old growth free.

For every 5,000 books printed, New Society saves the following resources:[1]

17	Trees
1,534	Pounds of Solid Waste
1,688	Gallons of Water
2,202	Kilowatt Hours of Electricity
2,789	Pounds of Greenhouse Gases
12	Pounds of HAPs, VOCs, and AOX Combined
4	Cubic Yards of Landfill Space

[1]Environmental benefits are calculated based on research done by the Environmental Defense Fund and
other members of the Paper Task Force who study the environmental impacts of the paper industry.

For a full list of NSP's titles, please call 1-800-567-6772 or check out our web site at:

www.newsociety.com

new society
PUBLISHERS